MW01121484

Radical
Criminology

issue one ★ fall 2012

ISSN: 1929-7904
ISBN: 978-0615695877

a publication of the
Critical Criminology Working Group
at Kwantlen Polytechnic University
(12666 - 72 Avenue, Surrey, BC V3W 2M8)
www.radicalcriminology.org

punctum books ✳ **brooklyn, ny**
http://www.punctumbooks.com

★ Radical Criminology ★ Issue 1 ★ November 2012 ★ ISSN 1929-7904

General Editor: Jeff Shantz

Production Editor: PJ Lilley

Advisory Board: Davina Bhandar (Trent U.); Jeff Ferrell (Texas Christian U.); Hollis Johnson, (Kwantlen Polytechnic U.); Mike CK Ma, (Kwantlen Polytechnic U.); Lisa Monchalin, (Kwantlen Polytechnic U.); Heidi Rimke, (U.Winnipeg); Jeffrey Ian Ross, (U.Baltimore)

cover art: Milica Ružičić

layout & design: PJ Lilley

Unless otherwise stated, contributions express the opinions of their writers and are not (necessarily) those of the Editors or Advisory Board. Please visit our website for more information.

★ Contact Us ★

email: editors@radicalcriminology.org

website: http://journal.radicalcriminology.org

Mailing address: Kwantlen Polytechnic University, ATTN: Jeff Shantz, Dept. of Criminology 12666 72 Avenue I Surrey, BC, Canada V3W 2M8

★

In this period of state-sponsored austerity and suppression of resistance there is a great need for criminologists to speak out and act against state violence, state-corporate crime, and the growth of surveillance regimes and the prison-industrial complex. Criminologists also have a role to play in advancing alternatives to current regimes of regulation and punishment. In light of current social struggles against neo-liberal capitalism, and as an effort to contribute positively to those struggles, the Critical Criminology Working Group at Kwantlen Polytechnic University in Vancouver has initiated this open access journal, *Radical Criminology*. We now welcome contributions. (See back page or our website for more details.)

Future issues might include:
Prison Abolition • Anti-colonialism • Resistance to Borders & Securitization • Surveillance and the Digital Panopticon • Anti-capitalism & Corporate Crime • the Military-Industrial Complex

This is not simply a project of critique, but is geared toward a praxis of struggle, insurgence and practical resistance.

★

Readers are welcome, and contributors are requested, to keep in touch by signing up at
http://journal.radicalcriminology.org

Our website uses the Open Journal System,
developed by the Public Knowledge Project at
Simon Fraser University:
journal.radicalcriminology.org

Here, you may create your own profile to contribute to this
project, or simply subscribe your email address to our low traffic
mailing list, to receive notifications of important new content
added to the journal. Use of your address is limited to matters
relating to the journal, and we will not be sharing our
subscribers list with other organizations.

As an online, open access publication,
all our content is freely available to all researchers
worldwide ensuring maximum dissemination.

Printed paper copies with full color cover
are available at cost through

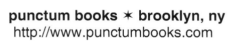

punctum books ✷ brooklyn, ny
http://www.punctumbooks.com

"SPONTANEOUS ACTS OF SCHOLARLY COMBUSTION"

punctum books is an "open-access and print-on-
demand independent publisher dedicated to radically
creative modes of intellectual inquiry and writing
across a whimsical para-humanities assemblage."

Inside

editorial /

features /

arts /

Radical Criminology: A Manifesto

In this period of state-sponsored austerity and suppression of resistance there is a great need for criminologists to speak out and act against state violence, state-corporate crime, and the growth of surveillance regimes and the prison-industrial complex. Criminologists also have a role to play in advancing alternatives to current regimes of regulation and punishment. In light of current social struggles against neo-liberal capitalism, and as an effort to contribute positively to those struggles, the Critical Criminology Working Group at Kwantlen Polytechnic University in Vancouver has initiated the journal *Radical Criminology*. We hope you will enjoy our first issue and find it to be a useful resource.

The present period represents an era of state capitalist offensives against the working classes and oppressed globally. It is played out in specific local maneuvers but is global in character. The main thrusts are austerity policies mean to break the infrastructures and resources on which the working classes and oppressed rely and to weaken possibilities for resistance and make people desperate and despairing. Conditions of austerity are effected through social and economic policies that limit the rights of workers on the labor market and at work and which remove alternatives to waged labor (such as welfare or low cost education). Along with austerity is the creation of crises and manufactured fear in the political fantasies of contagion (by terrorism, radicalism, or the foreign outsider). This fear is used to legitimize the deployment of repressive policies and practices (aggressive laws and policing patterns).

This is also an era in which the previous models of social change and resistance—notably Marxism/Leninism and the vanguard party, national liberation, and social democracy—have been discredited and/or discarded. New generations of people, with no particular prejudices, biases, or commitments toward the radical political models of the past and their associated claims on rightness (and righteousness) have become politicized on new terms and from new beginnings. This poses both great possibilities and great perils. On the one hand, there is the danger of starting over from scratch—of needlessly making the same mistakes that experience might avoid, of reinventing the wheel (as a flat tire), of pursuing false leads and getting caught in dead ends (reformism and adventurism, statism and electoralism, guerrilla moralism and vanguardism).

On the other hand, and more hopefully, there is the real possibility that new and more effective approaches will be developed, refined, and pursued. Forgotten voices and lost wisdom will once again be engaged in meaningful ways. This is already being realized in the widespread, and growing, engagement with anarchism, indigenous thinking, radical unionism, syndicalism, and horizontalism and direct action.

This period poses new challenges for intellectual workers, particularly academic social scientists. The challenges for criminologists (and criminology more broadly as a discipline) are even more pressing given that this is a period marked largely by punitive advances of capital and its (neo)liberal democratic management regimes. Criminal justice systems, and their diverse institutions, have been key weapons in the capitalist offensive against the working classes and oppressed. Criminologists, perhaps more than other social scientists, have an obligation to take a stand against the assaults of states on populations made increasingly vulnerable by the actions of economic and political powerholders.

It is now absolutely essential, as a matter of struggles for justice and against repression and criminalization, that criminologists take a firm and open stand against criminal justice policies and practices that serve capital at the expense of the working classes and oppressed. A radical criminology must act in solidarity with those individuals and groups targeted by the institutions of the state.

Radical criminology must not flinch in the face of condemnation by corporate mass media and political institutions. It is not enough to be a public criminologist. Criminology must go further to be an active, indeed an interested, player in contemporary struggles. Criminology must choose sides. It must stand with the movements of the exploited and against the exploiters. It must stand with the oppressed and against the oppressors. It must stand with the marginalized and against those who would claim (or impose) the privileged center. It must stand with the criminalized and against those who would criminalize them.

This discussion offers merely a sketch of some of the possible contours of a radical criminology. It is not meant as a final answer, but rather as an opening question.

OUTLINES OF A RADICAL CRIMINOLOGY

1. Radical criminology must be anti-statist and anti-capitalist. It must not succumb to the myth, as libertarians do, that there is an opposition between capitalism and the state. The emergence, development, and continuance of capitalism have been entirely facilitated by state practices. Indeed, capitalism is unimaginable without the state. The expropriation of land, enclosure of commons, defense of privatized property, and repression of peasant and working class opposition—the very foundations of capitalism—are all acts of the state. Without the repressive apparatuses of the state, capitalism would quickly collapse. The idea that the state and capitalist market are oppositional forces is falsity that serves only to distort history and confuse matters.

Capitalism is founded on the dual mechanisms of force and law. Criminal justice systems deploy legal means to sanction the forced theft of land and labor.

Legislative and material violence are the twin foundations of criminal justice systems. From the Enclosure Acts in England and the military violence used to impose them through the legislative foundations of slavery, colonialism, and genocide to the anti-panhandling and poor laws and social cleansing of today, these dual features are deployed against poor and working class communities (often on racialized terms).

2. A radical criminology must again recognize exploitation —the social exploitation of labor—as the central organizing feature of capitalist societies. The underlying motive force of the economy, exploitation provides the *raison d'être* of liberal democratic governance—that is ensuring and extending the conditions of exploitation of labor by capital. This too provides the impetus of criminal justice system policies and procedures since the earliest days of liberal democratic government. This has always been the foundation of criminal justice systems in liberal democracies. This is at the heart of these systems. Such practices have been central components of criminal justice practices from the start. Examples include the various poor laws and anti-vagrancy acts as well as state work camps and prison workhouses.

3. Criminal justice systems are themselves profit maximizing machines. The manner of their profit-making is the processing and punishment of the poor. Without the criminalization of the poor—as poor—criminal justice systems in Western liberal democracies would collapse or wither on the vine. In Canada, around 10% of the population live under the poverty line (even more are actually poor). Yet, the poor make up nearly 100% of incarcerated people.

Policing is primarily a racket for soft crime mining. They pan for crime in poor neighborhoods (typically after instigating or stoking moral panics to criminalize harmless activities like squeegeeing or panhandling from which they can then profit by pursuing) to keep arrest rates and crime stats higher and thus justify appeals for greater spending on their services.

And the cost of policing in times of austerity, which is no small expense, shows the hypocrisy of governments that claim tight budgets and limited funding for social services. In Vancouver, for example, the police account for around 21% of the City budget. This expense is rising and politically untouchable as far as possible cuts are concerned.

The single act of issuing one anti-panhandling ticket to a homeless person sets in motion a money-making assembly line of punishment and profit. Along the way various sectors of the system receive (unequal) payment which represents a transfer of wealth upwards (as the taxes of the working classes are transferred to the state agencies). First, there are the police officers who issue the tickets. Then there are the lawyers, bailiffs, judges, and jail or prison guards (to say nothing of the lower status court workers such as clerks and stenographers). At the end are the subsequent demands for more police and prisons to deal with "the problem." Prison construction companies, corporate food services, prison industries (slave labor firms) all follow along. Without this profitable foundation in the punishment of the poor the system of state capitalist criminal justice could not persist. Police, court, and prison budgets would lose their prop. At the same time we should not assume as liberals often do that diverted funds would be put toward socially necessary ends such as schools or hospitals.

This point is reinforced by the fact that 21% of charges in Canada are administration of justice charges such as failure to appear or boundary violations. Warrants and jail result from what was initially a minor charge due to the piling on of administrative charges (processing charges).

4. The state is a protection racket. That is its basic function. As with smaller gangs, the state leans on the population with displays of violence in a way to extract finances and support for "services rendered." More people have been killed by states than by all of the street gangs, thugs, Mafioso, hooligans, and terrorists in history combined.

5. Radical criminology must be anti-colonial. It must confront the historic and ongoing assaults on indigenous communities globally by settler capitalist states and their criminal justice systems. Radical criminology must be clear in stating that criminal justice systems in settler democracies are founded in practices of colonialism. Not only has legislation been utilized to dispossess indigenous communities of their land and resources and displace them from traditional territories. Laws have dismantled indigenous systems of governance and community self-determination. Practices like slavery, also have legal underpinnings. The programs of cultural genocide unleashed against indigenous communities were founded in legislation and legal institutions. They were never against the law.

Criminal justice processes are part of ongoing colonial strategies of containment and extinguishment directed toward indigenous communities. Native people account for 4% of the population in Canada but make up 20% of those incarcerated. Policing, surveillance, and incarceration serve as successors to more blatant programs of cultural genocide such as residential schools. Presently, 41% of native people who are incarcerated are under the age of 25.

Capitalist economies and liberal democratic governments are founded on expansionist practices (and policies) of enclosure. The history of colonial states is a history of displacement, land theft, murder, and genocide—all legally sanctioned and normalized. The impetus is the opening up of new areas of profitability and economic opportunities for capital. This is the real and integral character of state capitalist liberal democracies.

These are not anomalies or digressions or mistakes or unfortunate features of less enlightened times. These are the pillars of capitalist economies and liberal democratic justice systems. Without such practices—the forced acquisition of cheap land and labor and the breaking of communal bonds—capitalism could not have developed. State capitalism requires, from the start, the dislocation of local communities and their sustenance systems and governance practices.

Radical criminology must stand on the side of indigenous communities that fight back and reclaim their lands as in the case of Six Nations in Ontario and the Secwepemc struggles in British Columbia.

6. Radical criminology must challenge national sovereignty and border controls by statist institutions. It must reject the statist construction of migrants as legal versus "illegal." No one is illegal must be a clarion call for a radical criminology.

7. Radical criminology must be deep green. It must draw attention to and oppose the integral relationships between capitalist exploitation, business practices, and the destruction of the planet's various ecosystems. It must also highlight the complicity of states and capital in this destruction and call out the refusal of states to hold economic elites accountable for the harms they perpetrate against human communities and nature. Too often criminology has focused on the low level crimes of non-elites. Harms have been constructed as violations of laws or impacts on individuals or their property. Radical criminology must shift focus to the harmful activities of corporations and businesses (and the people who direct them) which are often not criminalized or "against the law." Radical criminologists must confront the hegemonic construction of the harm done by capital as simply part of business as usual. This includes confronting economic and political elites on the damage done to ecosystems, non-human nature, and other species—impacts that states and capital excuse as being mere externalities, part of the cost of doing business.

At the same time radical environmentalists, animal rights activists, and advocates of dark green resistance have been heavily targeted by states for criminalization. The repression of green activists today echoes the repression of anarchists and socialists during the Red Scare of the 1910s. Green activists have been subjected to lengthy prison sentences and their groups subjected to intense surveillance. In cases such as the bombing of green syndicalist Judi Bari, in which the Federal Bureau of Investigation (FBI) was involved, liberal democratic states have attempted to assassinate green activists. In addition, states in countries like the US have, under the guise of anti-terror concerns, devised laws to protect corporations from criticism for their ecologically destructive practices. These laws have been used to target even informational groups like Stop Huntington Animal Cruelty which simply try to expose corporate practices. In Canada the Minister of the Environment has labeled opponents of pipelines carrying tar sands oil as extremists in an effort to discredit them. Radical criminology must oppose the criminalization of green activists and point to the state complicity with capital motivating repressive measures against environmentalists.

8. Radical criminology is abolitionist; it must call for the abolition of all statist criminal justice systems. Systems of domination and exploitation cannot be reformed; there is no legitimate basis for reform or revision of policies and practices that are at heart founded in and based upon exploitation. There is no reasonable level of oppression. It is not enough to criticize such systems. Radical criminology must oppose and confront all statist institutions of criminal justice with an eye toward ending them. Such too is the case for institutions and relationships of capitalist exploitation.

PRACTICE

A. There is a pressing urgency that radical criminologists get out of the offices and into the streets and communities in which struggles are occurring. We must put ourselves on the line to stand in solidarity with people in the communities and workplaces in which our campuses and offices are located.

B. We should also recognize that campuses are also sites of exploitation and struggle. Radical criminologists should oppose the corporatization of our various intellectual labours, including teaching as well as research. Among our efforts radical criminologists need to fight neoliberal policies that turn universities and colleges into prep schools for corporate expansion and financial markets.

This means opposing recruitment efforts by police, border services, prisons, private security firms, as well as the military on our campuses. It also means opposing attempts by co-operative education offices to determine curriculum and turn programs into mere training grounds for institutions of repression.

C. A radical criminology needs to refuse the false dichotomies of legal/illegal protest, of violence/non-violence, of legitimate/illegitimate resistance. In state capitalist societies violence is a constant reality of everyday life. Typically it is experienced disproportionately in working class and poor communities whose members are subjected to economic violence at work (and on the labor market), social and cultural violence in schools and in media portrayals, and political violence in policing and criminal justice system practices that punish them overwhelmingly (indeed, almost exclusively). To preach non-violent resistance in such a context is to justify the continuance of state and corporate violence and deny working class and poor people the dignity of self-defense.

In the wake of the popular mobilizations against the economic and political elites of the G8 and G20 meetings in Ontario during the summer of 2010, even noted critical commentators firmly situated on the activist Left called for police repression of more militant activists, particularly anarchists and the so-called black blocs of people supporting and engaged in direct actions against corporate and government targets. Naomi

Klein infamously called on police in Toronto to do their "god-damned jobs" and protect property or arrest people intent on damaging property.

Even commentators long influenced by Marxism joined the chorus calling for the arrests of anarchists and others engaged in (or threatening to engage in) direct action. Judy Rebick, Sam Gindin Chair in Social Justice at Ryerson University and rabble.ca founder, suggested police should have preemptively arrested militant activists and angry residents involved in property destruction. Unfortunately, her plea was unnecessary as police had already done by arresting several prominent anarchist activists in the days prior to the G20 meetings in Toronto. Those committed organizers had their lives placed in turmoil for over a year and some received lengthy jail terms for having done nothing more than discuss the possibility of direct actions (in contexts in which police infiltrators were present). Thus the wish for preemptive arrests—which has no place among critical theorists or activists—had already been carried out.

Notions of legality and illegality reflect the priorities of states and capital and should not be the basis for assessing movements of resistance. In discussions of legalism/illegalism the state and its corporate backers set the terms of debate. Against statist definitions of ill/legality radical criminologists must assert the needs of people and their environments (including natural environments and their non-human occupants).

D. Property damage is not violence. Only a profoundly unjust society privileges property over the needs of people. Only a distorted system of justice allows property owners to sit on useable housing while arresting those who break into such property to meet their life and death needs for housing. These are the expression of specific decisions to protect property at the expense of human need.

On the other hand, abandoned workplaces do reflect acts of violence. Similarly, foreclosed homes.

E. Radical criminology must break down the barriers between inside and outside. Criminologists need to give explicit support to political prisoners criminalized for their engagement in social justice struggles, resistance, or revolutionary activities. This includes material support (such as prison visits, setting up books to prisoners programs, publishing prisoners' works) as well as speaking publicly in defense of political prisoners and the state practices of repression deployed against them. Radical criminologists must work to show that economic prisoners are also political prisoners. Economic crimes of the poor and working classes result from political decisions and the preferences and choices of economic and political elites. Laws, policing, and prisons are political to the core. Those who are victimized by such political practices are by definition political prisoners.

Once again a radical criminology does not base support on legal judgments of the actions for which political prisoners have been criminalized. Again, we do not privilege some political prisoners over others on a statist basis of violence or non-violence. We do not withdraw support on the basis that a political prisoner has engaged in or advocated armed struggle, property destruction, or the violation of laws. We cannot allow ourselves to be sectarian in working with or supporting political prisoners. Political differences can be dealt with in direct discussion and debate. As the Industrial Workers of the World (IWW) used to say: "They're in there for us; we're out here for them."

F. Radical criminology must be proactive in pursuing workable alternatives to statist forms of criminal justice. Indeed the notion of "criminal justice" should probably be discarded altogether. Radical criminologists have already innovated and advocated for various real world alternatives. These include restorative justice outside of statist institutions as well as healing circles. There are many overlooked, silenced, ignored, and suppressed traditions and tendencies that radical criminology can draw from and build upon. Indigenous governance practices have contributed much toward alternative understandings of communal justice and practical alternative relations. Radical criminology needs a deep and close engagement with indigenous experiences of governance. More work must be done in developing and pursuing community and workplace self defense practices.

G. Radical criminology must be prepared to oppose authoritarian manifestations within our own movements and organizations. We do not need a vanguard party or wannabe states-information within our own ranks. The vast experiences of the twentieth century show rather starkly what a dead end such approaches, seductive though they might be for some, actually are. In any event, participants in the contemporary movements emerging globally are developing, experimenting with, and putting into practice alternative approaches. Radical criminologists will gain by engaging with, learning from, and debating those approaches. Among the important development of contemporary movements is the emphasis on horizontalism and participatory decision making.

Onward

A radical criminology should, in short, be an insurgent criminology. It should be a criminology that provides a useful resource for movements of resistance and communities in struggle against exploitation and oppression.

In times of crisis and intense social struggles—certainly in times of insurrection or uprising—radical criminologists must keep their heads and not succumb to moral backlash or fear, even of the Left and political progressives. It can be too easy for otherwise critical voices to lose confidence under the spotlight of state reaction and media outrage. In such times especially one must advance and sharpen—not lose or abandon—their politics.

Radical criminology is not simply a project of critique, but is geared toward a praxis of struggle, insurgence, and practical resistance. It is a criminology of direct action.

Jeff Shantz, Surrey, Summer 2012

nooneisillegal.org

[features]

Security Assemblages and Spaces of Exception: The Production of (Para-) Militarized Spaces in the U.S. War on Drugs

MARKUS KIENSCHERF,
THE FREE UNIVERSITY OF BERLIN

In a special issue of *Small Wars and Insurgencies*, specifically dedicated to the "drug wars' in the U.S.-Mexico borderlands, a number of contributors assert that Mexico is embroiled in a violent conflict both amongst drug cartels and between cartels and state security agencies, and may ultimately turn into a failed state (Bunker 2010; Bunker and Sullivan 2010). American law enforcement expert Robert Bunker, for instance, suggests that

> gang, cartel, and mercenary groups can translate a higher percentage of their economies (group revenue) into "criminal-insurgent' activities based on diplomacy-corruption (*plata*) and military-like (*plomo*) capabilities than the nation-state "law enforcement' capabilities needed to counter them. (2010, 21)

Bunker further argues that this has led to a situation in which the Mexican state "is no longer able to govern entire sectors within its sovereign territory and, instead, these areas have been taken by a narco-insurgency and lost to the influence of criminal-based entities' (2010, 10). Moreover, he contends that what he views as Mexico's "narco-insurgency' can quickly spread and mutate into a threat of hemispheric proportions (2010, 9-10).

On September 8, 2010 U.S. Secretary of State Hillary Clinton made similar claims about the situation in Mexico—much to the chagrin of Mexican officials:

> This is a really tough challenge. And these drug cartels are now showing more and more indices of insurgency; all of a sudden, car bombs show up which weren't there before. (Clinton 2010, n,p.)

Yet, this is merely the latest episode in a story that has been unfolding since the late 1960s. A few months after he took office in 1969, President Richard Nixon informed Congress about what he viewed as a new threat to the nation:

> Within the last decade, the abuse of drugs has grown from essentially a local police problem into a serious national threat to the personal health and safety of millions of Americans. [...] A national awareness of the gravity of the situation is needed: a new urgency and concerted national policy are needed at the federal level to begin to cope with this growing menace to the general welfare of the United States. (Nixon 1969, 57A)

Addressing the International Drug Enforcement Conference in Miami on April 27, 1989 President George H. W. Bush went a whole step further and equated the fight against drugs with a world war of epic proportions:

> I'm here today to talk about war: first, to see cocaine trafficking for what it is – an attack aimed at enslaving and exploiting the weak; second, to confront what's become a world war. [...] And I've said it before: The war on drugs is no metaphor. We've been slower to recognize that it is also a world war, leaving no nation unscathed, one in which Hong Kong bankers and Bolivian growers and Middle Eastern couriers and west coast wholesalers all play insidious roles. And it is especially acute in this hemisphere, where an explosive cycle of drugs, dependency, and dollars has escalated clear out of control. (Bush 1989, n.p.)

From the late 1960s the war on drugs has served to justify both a massive police build-up and increasing federal involvement in the hitherto predominantly local and regional domain of law enforcement. Moreover, the war on drugs meshed nicely with wide-ranging government efforts to crack down on increasingly militant domestic dissent. Christian Parenti even goes as far as to argue that the war on drugs and the ensuing overhaul of policing was primarily geared toward the suppression of domestic Black and Latino militancy (Parenti 1999). In a similar vein, when the war on drugs was exported abroad in the 1980s, it served as a justification for a permanent "U.S. counter-intelligence and paramilitary presence' (Bullington and Block 1990, 39; cf. Marshall 1987; Morales 1989). Although the war on drugs has recently been overshadowed by the war on terror, it has shaped U.S. domestic and foreign affairs for several decades and continues to do so. What is more the war on terror and the war on drugs have been increasingly folded into one another, driven by the putative threats of "narco-terrorism' or "narco-insurgency' (Bunker 2010; Bunker and Sullivan 2010; Kan 2009).

In this essay I will take a closer look at how the war on drugs has *para-militarized* space. I wish to briefly discuss three interrelated facets. Firstly, I will highlight how the war on drugs has been framed by the ambiguous logic of security, above all the blurring of the boundaries between policing and war-fighting. In fact, George H. W. Bush was right: the war on drugs was (and is) no metaphor. But it's not a conventional war either. The war on drugs is best understood by looking at the military doctrines that came to shape it: low-intensity conflict (LIC) and counterinsurgency (COIN) doctrine. Secondly, I will show how the war on drugs has subjected space to the logic of security. I will argue that this process has entailed the design and deployment of border regimes, not just in the sense of borders between sovereign states but also in terms of complex assemblages that allow for the distinction between legitimate and illegitimate flows of people and resources. I will argue that these security assemblages serve tactically to enact a strategic sovereign decision on the legitimacy or illegitimacy of people and goods. Thirdly, I will discuss the international dimension of the war on drugs, how it has been folded into counterinsurgency operations in Latin America, most notably through Plan Colombia, and how it is now folded into the war on terror.

SECURITY

The traditional dividing line between crime and war has become increasingly fuzzy. This is encapsulated in the ambiguous logic of security. Above all, security blurs the distinction between policing and war-fighting and the concomitant boundaries between inside and outside. Eyal Weizman provides a concise summary of this ambiguity:

> The logic of "security' [...] presupposes that the danger is already inside, presented by a population in which subversive elements exist. [...] If defence engages directly with the concept of war, security engages with the temporarily ill-defined and spatially amorphous "conflict' not only between societies, but within them as well. "Security' conceives new spatial practices and arrangements. It erects barriers and channels and rechannels the flow of people and resources through space. According to the logic of security, only a constantly configured and reconfigured environment is a safe environment. (Weizman 2007, 106-107)

Security centres around the management of flows of people and resources by means of configuring and re-configuring space. These configurations of space are based on a form of risk management. Risk is viewed as something that affects certain populations more than others. Moreover, particular populations and spaces are identified, categorized, and ultimately targeted as both at-risk and risky. In the context of the war on drugs, certain populations are considered to be more at risk of becoming victims of drugs and drug-related crime and more risky in the sense of harbouring threats against others. For example, U.S. domestic counter-narcotics efforts hinge on identifying so-called crime hotspots where drugs are sold to end users and where drug-related crime rates are particularly high. These hotspots are more likely than not located in poor urban and mostly Black or Latino neighbourhoods. These neighbourhoods are then subjected to high-intensity, or rather para-militarized, policing that, above all, seeks to contain the risks associated with drug-related activities, ensuring that they don't spill over into white, middle-class neighbourhoods. At the same time, the increasing fortification of the U.S.-Mexico border is also aimed at containing risky populations and activities, ensuring that they don't flow into the homeland.

The war on drugs has been "America's longest running concept war' (Bewley-Taylor 2005, 84). According to David R. Bewley-Taylor, "concept wars' are wars waged against an abstract concept, such as drugs or terrorism, rather than against a concrete enemy. Concept wars tend to be open-ended. As Bewley-Taylor puts it, "the absence of an enemy that can offer unconditional surrender, has the potential to produce perpetual conflict' (2005, 104). Allen Feldman refers to these conflicts as "securocratic wars of public safety':

> These wars are not exclusively focused on territorial conquest, or on an easily locatable or identifiable enemy with its own respective goals of territorial appropriation. Rather, they are focused on countering imputed territorial contamination and transgression – "terrorist', demographic and biological infiltration. These campaigns are not structured by time-limited political goals but are temporally open-ended. (Feldman 2004, 331)

Due to their open-ended nature securocratic wars amount to a permanent state of exception that erodes the conceptual boundaries between war and peace, law and violence, war-fighting and policing. Securocratic warfare, the amorphous notion of security and the state of exception form a tightly concatenated ensemble of power that cuts across the traditional boundaries between the domestic and the foreign arena and, at same time, constantly (re-)produces distinctions between those who belong and those who have to be excluded or even eliminated.

Through the war on drugs both border control and the policing of what sociologist Loïc Wacquant calls hyperghettos have become saturated with military hardware, expertise and doctrine (2001). However, it wouldn't be entirely accurate to speak of a militarization of policing. Since the war on drugs has eroded the very boundaries between policing and war-fighting, it has also led to what we may call the "policization' of the military. To an ever larger extent, the U.S. military has been urged to take on constabulary and policing missions. In short, the U.S. armed forces have been enjoined to play a more and more prominent role in controlling civilian populations both domestically and abroad[1]. I think we should rather speak of the paramilitarization of both domestic and foreign social control, because this process is not so much informed by the doctrines of conventional inter-state warfare, as by low-intensity conflict and counterinsurgency doctrines.

Allen Feldman suggests that domestic policing has morphed into "a variation of counterinsurgency as crime is increasingly administered and contoured as a mode of clandestine economic circulation' (2004, 334). Policing is concerned with the preemptive identification, tracking and targeting of illegitimate

---

[1] We should, however, note that this trend is also the subject of much debate and controversy, especially amongst military top brass.

flows of people and goods that blend into the quotidian circulation of legitimate flows. In this respect, domestic policing faces the same challenges as counterinsurgency: while counterinsurgents have to identify insurgents who hide amongst civilian populations, police forces have to identify potential and actual criminals as well as contraband amongst the legitimate everyday activities of ordinary people.

Irregular warfare[2] is indeed characterized by a fuzzy relation between foreign defence and domestic public safety, the "policization' of the military and the militarization of the police, and an emphasis on so-called pacification or population control (Army 2007; Dunn 1996; Kienscherf 2010; Long 2006; Ucko 2009). The fact that these types of warfare are focussed on the control of civilians is of particular relevance here:

> The larger objective of LIC [low-intensity conflict] doctrine is to effect social control over targeted civilian populations by drawing selectively from this vast continuum of tactics to address any threat to stability (from a broad range of security concerns) in a manner that theoretically is more judicious and appropriate than are heavy-handed, less discriminate, conventional military approaches (Dunn 1996, 148).

In his book on *The New Counterinsurgency Era* David Ucko maintains that counterinsurgency and stability operations share three significant features: (1) they occur in a context of hostile activity (also known as a nonpermissive operational environment); (2) the stabilization effort forms part of a wider state-building initiative; and (3) the stabilizing force is deployed in the midst of a civilian population (Ucko 2009, 9-11). To a certain extent, the deployment of military tactics, technologies and troops in the war on drugs exhibits all these features.

First of all, the Reagan, Bush, and Clinton administrations massively escalated the war on drugs, turning it from a rhetorical device aimed at marshalling both public opinion and resources into an actual low-intensity conflict that was (and still is) fought not only along the U.S.-Mexico border but also in the streets of America's hyperghettos. Dunn, for instance, quotes a leading federal counter-narcotics official[3], who at the beginning

---

[2]   In fact, many of the differences between counterinsurgency operations, low-intensity conflict, or stability operations are largely about shifting trends in military jargon.

[3]   The name of the official is Warren Reece, then coordinator of the Southwest Border High Intensity Drug-Trafficking Area Program and director of Operation Alliance. Operation Alliance was an extensive federal counter-narcotics effort involving a

of the nineties baldly stated, "We are engaged in something akin to a guerrilla war along the border against well-entrenched and well-organized trafficking groups' (Dunn 1996, 3). Moreover, the 1980s saw a spate of raids and ghetto sweeps in which heavily armed paramilitary police arrested thousands of, mostly black, young men. For example, in April 1988 the Los Angeles Police Department (LAPD) launched Operation HAMMER, "arresting more black youth than at any other time since the Watts Rebellion of 1965" (Davis 1992, 267-8). In fact, in the late 1980s and early 1990s Los Angeles was gripped by a massive anti-gang frenzy, as gangs came to be seen as the chief distribution networks for crack cocaine:

> In the official version, which Hollywood is incessantly reheating and further sensationalizing these gangs comprise veritable urban guerrilla armies organized for the sale of crack and outgunning the police with huge arsenals of UZI and Mac-10 automatics. Although gang cohorts are typically hardly more than high-school sophomores, local politicians frequently compare them to the "murderous militias of Beirut." (Davis 1992, 268)

A local mayor even went as far as to refer to gang members as "the Viet Cong abroad in our society" (Davis 1992, 268). Ever since drugs were declared a threat to national security, drug trafficking has been habitually scripted as a hostile activity that mandates the deployment of a wide range of security assets. Swaths of the border region as well as certain inner-city neighbourhoods have thus regularly been designated as quasi-hostile environments[4].

Secondly, considering the deployment of military tactics, technologies and personnel both along the border and in domestic hyperghettos as part of a wider attempt at state-building may, at first glance, seem like a bit of a stretch. However, we have to bear in mind that on a more general level border regimes have always played a major part in state-making. As Mexico's own domestic war on drugs heated up and turned more and more violent, with 7,200 victims of drug-related violence in 2008 alone, a Pentagon report, published in November 2008, concluded that due to the "sustained assault and pressure

---

number of different law enforcement agencies supported by the military (Dunn 1996: 200n).

[4] For instance, in 1990 a 150-mile area along the southwest border was declared a "High-Intensity-Drug-Trafficking Area" (alongside four other sites located in major cities) (Dunn 1996: 112).

by criminal gangs' Mexico's government, police and judicial structures might collapse turning Mexico into a failed state" (USJFC 2008, 40). While a number of senior intelligence officials disputed the report's claims, the newly elected Obama administration responded to the study's warnings that "an unstable Mexico could represent a homeland security problem of immense proportions to the United States" by drawing up a "multi-agency security plan for the border" (Hsu and Sheridan 2009).The particular configuration of the border regime is a chief factor in the (re-)production of national identity, to the extent that it produces the on-the-ground distinction between who (and what) is to be included and who (and what) is to be excluded from the imagined community of the nation(-state). From this point of view, fighting a war on drugs both along national borders and in domestic "hotspots" can indeed be seen as a stability operation that forms part of a wider exercise in state-making[5].

Thirdly and most importantly, the para-militarization of counter-narcotics efforts occurs in the midst of a civilian population that is sought to be controlled and managed, in order to identify dangerous elements hiding amongst the quotidian circulation of legitimate flows.

SPACE

On the one hand, populations are controlled through intelligence-led tactics, such as raids, terry stops, search-and-seizure operations, saturation patrols, etc.—tactics that we see both in counterinsurgency operations and in the context of domestic policing. On the other hand, control over targeted populations is effected through configuring space in such a way that flows of people and resources can be managed more effectively. This can take the form of barriers, road blocks, motion sensors, CCTV cameras, or more subtle urban design features that signal

---

[5]   We should also note that border interdiction is commonly seen as a staple of counterinsurgency and stability operations insofar as it seeks to deny insurgents vital supplies as well as cross-border sanctuary (Celeski 2006; Long 2006). As retired U.S. Army Colonel Joseph Celeski puts it, "Porous borders and spaces for sanctuary, which provide operating space, can prolong an insurgency if the counterinsurgent ignores them or handles them insufficiently' (Celeski 2006, 51). Celeski further describes border areas in which insurgents operate as "ungoverned spaces' that have to be brought under government control (Celeski 2006).

to risky populations that they are not welcome in certain areas. Tactics, physical changes in the environment and forms of knowledge(-production) are assembled into complex security mechanisms. These mechanisms face the seemingly impossible task of facilitating the smooth movement of shoppers, travellers, and commodities while filtering out criminals, terrorists, "illegal aliens" and contraband.

The construal of speed and mobility as defining characteristics of late modernity has almost become a cliché of contemporary social theory. Indeed, in the over-hyped accounts of a borderless world brought about by technology, transportation and economic globalization, the border is a generally under-theorized and under-studied site of contemporary politics (Zureik and Salter 2005, 5). Yet Zureik and Salter suggest that "[i]nter-state borders—of various significance—are central to the global mobility regime, the international system in both political and economic spheres, and to national identity. Inter-state frontiers always reflect the over-determination of economic, military, and cultural boundaries" (2005, 3).

However, besides demarcating national territory, borders are complex assemblages of tactics, technologies, and forms of knowledge(-production) that serve as instruments for tracking, targeting and managing the flow of people, goods and information in space. Border assemblages ought to be understood as sorting mechanisms that (re-)produce a distinction between legitimate and illegitimate elements and inscribe it in space. Due to a massive rise in mobility, borders can no longer be thought of in terms of traditional points of entry that allow movement into and out of a clearly demarcated territory. As Mark Salter argues:

> From the macro-politics of inside / outside, we see the emergence of a micro-politics of surveillance nets and vulnerable nodes. Thus, we have seen a sea change in our notion of territoriality, wherein the anxiety which was previously centred on the border has been projected onto a set of internal security measures (such as airport security and mall surveillance). (2005, 41-2)

Indeed, hardening "targets' such as shopping malls, train stations, airports and other (semi-)public spaces ought to be seen as a set of micro-level techniques geared toward (re-)producing the macro-level distinction between who belongs and who does not. In short, border regimes are micro-political assemblages aimed at resolving the macro-political tension between geo-e-conomic and geo-political imperatives; that is to say, border regimes are designed to produce and reinforce a sovereign distinction between flows whose movement needs to be facilitated and those that need to be interdicted (Lahav 2008; Lyon 2008; Salter 2005, 2008a, 2008b; Sparke 2006).

Border assemblages are concrete manifestations of the liberal governmental technology that Michel Foucault called "apparatuses of security." Foucault saw freedom of movement as instrumental for the operation of security within liberal governmentality:

> I think it is this freedom of circulation, in the broad sense of the term, it is in terms of this option of circulation, that we should understand the word freedom, and understand it as one of the facets, aspects, or dimensions of the deployment of apparatuses of security. (2007, 48-9)

But not everybody or everything has this "option of circulation", or has it to the same extent. In fact, some people are taken out of circulation completely. Rates of incarceration in the U.S. are staggering. According to the Bureau of Justice Statistics, in 2008 the U.S. correctional population, that is to say, those in prison, jail, on parole or on probation totaled 7.3 million. About 36% of the prison and jail population was black, 34% was white and 20% Hispanic (Justice 2009, 2). Black males are still six and a half times more likely to end up in jail than white males. By and large, the constant rise in the number of Americans under some form of correctional supervision is a direct consequence of the war on drugs.

Moreover, according to Loïc Wacquant, the prison and the hyperghetto constitute two increasingly intertwined sites for the confinement of a highly racialized criminal underclass considered to pose a risk to white, middle-class society (2001). The hyperghetto and the prison are instruments for controlling risky populations. But they also constitute risky spaces that, due to the very fact that they warehouse risky populations, need to be constantly monitored, controlled, policed and targeted by a variety of different tactics and technologies, ranging from methods of environmental design to the use of paramilitary police units. In short, they are spaces of exception that are not governed according to liberal standards.

The distinction between *liberal* and *illiberal* flows is the defining characteristic of a fundamental, albeit often disavowed, sovereign decision inherent in liberal governmentality. In this context the term sovereign distinction refers to the persistence of a specific form of sovereign power within governmentality. In the literature on governmentality sovereignty is defined as the exercise of central authority through the institutions of law and the executive. Governmentality, on the other hand, consists of a variety of decentred strategies and tactics aimed at promoting socio-economic processes. (Butler 2004; Dean 1999, 2000, 2002; Gordon 1991; Hindess 2004). Liberal governmentality emerged from a critique of an excess of government said to stifle these vital processes. It seeks to delimit the legitimate scope of government through the promotion of individual liberty and autonomy more effectively to foster and manage the socio-economic processes of the population (Dean 1999, 2000; Hindess 2004). Yet not everybody is seen as capable of exercising his or her liberty and some are even considered threats to the very existence of the liberal order. Thus, sovereignty is redeployed within the field of governmentality and assumes the function of an executive decision as to who or what constitutes a threat to the free development of society's vital processes (Agamben 1995, 2005). This is a decision on the exception(s), a decision as to who can be governed through the promotion of freedom and who needs to be governed in a more authoritarian fashion (Hindess 2004). In fact, liberal governmentality hinges on a distinction between those who can be governed liberally and those who must be governed through illiberal or coercive means (Corva 2008, 177; Hindess 2004, 28). Sovereignty persists and even multiplies within the field of liberal governmentality (cf. Agamben 1995; 2002; 2005). But it no longer occupies a clearly identifiable position at the centre of government (cf. Butler 2004, 50-100). Rather, sovereignty has become decentred; it now pervades the entire social field and manifests itself in all those multiform and variegated governmental mechanisms that are geared toward distinguishing between liberal and illiberal elements.

The two most fundamental illiberal regimes of liberal governmentality are "the application of the military apparatus (the strategy of warfare) and the application of the criminal justice apparatus (the strategy of policing citizens)' (Corva 2008, 177). And as liberal governmentality now increasingly centres on the identification and targeting of *both* domestic *and* foreign spaces and populations of exception, these two illiberal regimes have become more and more indistinguishable (Corva 2008):

> From the favelas of Rio de Janeiro to the slums of Mexico City to the shantytowns of Port-au-Prince; from the Andean highlands to Central American *milpas*; from Bogota's adolescent assassins to Los Angeles-El Salvador Mara Salvatrucha gangmembers; from New York's "zero tolerance" policing to Guatemala's "Mano extra-dura" policing, disposable spaces and subjects of neoliberal global-ization have been increasingly targeted by militarized police depart-ments, military forces, and paramilitary forces in the name of get-ting tough on crime – usually narcotics-related crime. This aug-mentation of the state's capacity to govern has occurred in tandem with the rolling back of its capacity to govern global capital through neoliberalization (Corva 2008, 177).

In short, specific spaces and populations are discursively con-structed as risks to the liberal order and hence as targets of illib-eral modes of government. And the instruments designed to tar-get these illiberal spaces and populations frequently take the form of para-militarized policing and/or border assemblages. As a consequence, the knowledge regimes that serve to identify and categorize illiberal subjects and the actual practices of tar-geting these illiberal subjects must be seen as integral parts of liberal governmentality – both domestically and internationally.

CRISSCROSSING DOMESTIC AND FOREIGN SPACES

Plan Colombia, which was launched by the Clinton adminis-tration in 1999, was a clear step toward a further escalation of the war on drugs. Plan Colombia folded counter-narcotics oper-ations into counterinsurgency and vice versa. In response to the killing of U.S. activists by FARC guerrillas, a general increase in guerrilla attacks and kidnappings in the wake of stalled peace talks between the FARC and the Colombian government, and the recognition that the seemingly successful kingpin strategy[6] had failed to stem the flow of drugs into the U.S., the Clinton administration decided to frame Colombian instability as a threat to national security (Crandall 2002: 162). Plan Colombia

---

[6] The so-called kingpin strategy was launched in 1992 to specifically target the heads of major, mainly Colombian, drugs cartels.

was above all about increasing both military assistance and humanitarian aid to the Colombian government. Thus, in many respects this policy was a counterinsurgency-style combination of security and development. But it was presented to Congress as a new chapter in the war on drugs because the White House was aware that if scripted as part of the war on drugs, few members of Congress would oppose Plan Colombia. The Clinton administration thus went to great lengths to stress that Plan Colombia was a counter-narcotics rather than a counterinsurgency initiative (Crandall 2002, 163).

Plan Colombia has now entered its twelfth year. In October 2009 the government of Colombia granted the Pentagon the use of seven military bases and a number of other smaller facilities. And Colombia still receives billions in military aid. According to Greg Grandin, Plan Colombia should be understood as "the Latin American edition of GCOIN, or Global Counterinsurgency' aimed at establishing a "unified, supra-national counterinsurgent infrastructure', in order to counter what Pentagon planners describe as a fusion between the drugs trade and global terrorism (2010, 9-11).

According to Paul Rexton Kan, associate professor of national security studies at the U.S. Army War College, "The drug trade and warfare have been pushed into a closer relationship by the lack of the overarching global superpower competition, asymmetrical nature of contemporary wars, changes in the patterns of the drug trade, and increasing pace of globalization' (2009, 94). Kan contends that in the future more and more conflicts will, therefore, be fuelled by the drugs trade. And this will likely give rise to an ever larger number of well-financed and hence also well-armed non-state war-making entities:

> [I]nternal or intrastate war is increasingly a misleading moniker. The emergence of organized violence no longer needs to anchor political authority in conventional, bureaucratic, or consent-based structures like the nation-state. The drug trade is speeding this process along. It too is neither dependent on nor bound by the nation-state and has over its history been less and less subject to a variety of local, national, and international enforcement capabilities (Kan 2009, 115).

For Kan, the increasingly close link between the drugs trade and warfare poses a significant challenge for Western nation states insofar as it erodes the distinction between public safety and national security. He argues that "[f]or the U.S. War on Terrorism, the implications are that it will be 'unsuccessful without integrating both "a war on drugs" and "a war on crime""" (2009, 144; quote from Marenko 2002, 63). A number of security pundits are now demanding that, due to the ever more intricate interrelations between drugs trafficking and violent conflict, counter-narcotics efforts should become an integral part of a global U.S. stabilization strategy (Kan 2009; Kilcullen 2005, 2009). This has given rise to the ultimate strategic goal of developing a deterritorialized homeland security capability of global proportions: a spatially and temporally indeterminate capability to execute a sovereign distinction between liberal and illiberal flows of people and resources. However, the U.S. is unlikely to achieve unconventional global military superiority on top of its often totally useless conventional military superiority.

CONCLUSION

The war on drugs in many ways already anticipated the next major U.S. securocratic war: the so-called war on terror. Like the war on terror America's drug war has proved both spatially and temporally indeterminate. What is more, it has eroded the distinction between war-fighting and policing and hence resulted in a complete intermingling of domestic and international security. Michael Hardt and Antonio Negri put it quite succinctly:

> In the context of this cross between military and police activity there is ever less difference between inside and outside the nation-state: low-intensity warfare meets high-intensity policing. The "enemy", which has traditionally been conceived outside, and the "dangerous classes," which have traditionally been inside, are thus increasingly indistinguishable from one another and serve together as the object of the war effort (2004, 14-15).

What Hardt and Negri call the "enemy" and the "dangerous classes" are those who are deemed impervious to liberal governance, those who are seen as a threat to liberalism and hence need to be either excluded from liberal society, or eliminated.

Ultimately, the illiberal subject positions produced by Western discourses and practices of security are empty placeholders that can be filled, depending on the political conjuncture, with a variety of categories: terrorists, insurgents, criminals, immigrants, the undeserving poor, or African Americans, Latinos or Muslims. What all these categories have in common is that they operate within the fundamental Manichaeism opened up by the sovereign decision on who has to be governed through authoritarian means. And this Manichaeism now increasingly operates across and beyond the divide between the domestic and the international sphere.

REFERENCES

Agamben, G. 1995. *Homo Sacer. Sovereign Power and Bare Life.* Translated by D. Heller-Roazen. Stanford: Stanford University Press.

———. 2002. "Security and Terror". *Theory and Event* 5 (4):1-2.

———. 2005. *The State of Exception.* Translated by K. Attell. Chicago: University of Chicago Press.

Army, U.S. Department of the. 2007. *The U.S. Army / Marine Corps Counterinsurgency Field Manual.* Chicago: University of Chicago Press.

Bewley-Taylor, D. 2005. "US concept wars, civil liberties and the technologies of fortification'. *Crime Law and Social Change* 43 (1):81-111.

Bullington, B., and A. A. Block. 1990. "A Trojan horse - Anti-communism and the war on drugs." *Contemporary Crises* 14 (1):39-55.

Bunker, Robert J. 2010. "Strategic threat: narcos and narcotics overview." *Small Wars & Insurgencies* 21 (1):8-29.

Bunker, Robert J., and John P. Sullivan. 2010. "Cartel evolution revisited: third phase cartel potentials and alternative futures in Mexico." *Small Wars & Insurgencies* 21 (1):30-54.

Bush, George H. W. 1989. "Remarks at the International Drug Enforcement Conference in Miami, Florida, April 27, 1989"; available at: http://bushlibrary.tamu.edu/research/public_papers.php?id=365&year=1989&month=4 (accessed 10/26/2009).

Butler, Judith. 2004. *Precarious Life: the Powers of Mourning and Violence.* London, New York: Verso.

Celeski, Joseph. 2006. "Attacking Insurgent Space: Sanctuary Denial and Border Interdiction." *Military Review* 86 (6):51-57.

Clinton, Hillary R. 2010. "Remarks on United States Foreign Policy"; *Speech at the Council of Foreign Relations* (September 8, 2010); available at: http://www.state.gov/secretary/rm/2010/09/146917.htm (accessed 9 September 2010).

Corva, D. 2008. "Neoliberal globalization and the war on drugs: Transnationalizing illiberal governance in the Americas." *Political Geography* 27 (2):176-193.

Crandall, R. 2002. "Clinton, Bush and Plan Colombia." *Survival* 44 (1):159-172.

Davis, Mike. 1992. *City of Quartz. Excavating the Future in Los Angeles.* New York: Vintage Books.

Dean, Mitchell. 1999. *Governmentality: Power and Rule in Modern Society*. Thousand Oaks: Sage Publications.

————. 2000. "Liberal government and authoritarianism." *Economy & Society* 31 (1):37-61.

————. 2002. "Powers of Life and Death Beyond Governmentality." *Cultural Values* 6 (1/2):119-138.

Dunn, T. J. 1996. *The Militarization of the U.S.-Mexico Border 1978-1992. Low-Intensity Conflict Doctrine Comes Home*. Austin, TX: Center for Mexican American Studies.

Feldman, Allen. 2004. "Securocratic Wars of Public Safety." *Interventions: The International Journal of Postcolonial Studies* 6 (3):330-350.

Foucault, Michel. 2007. *Security, Territory, Population. Lectures at the College de France 1977 -1978*. Translated by G. Burchell. Houndmills, Basingstoke: Palgrave Macmillan. Original edition, 2004.

Gordon, Colin. 1991. "Governmental Rationality". In *The Foucault Effect. Studies in Governmentality*, edited by G. Burchell, C. Gordon and P. Miller. Chicago: University of Chicago Press.

Grandin, Greg. 2010. "Muscling Latin America". *The Nation* February 8, 2010:9-13.

Hardt, Michael, and Antonio Negri. 2004. *Multitude. War and Democracy in the Age of Empire*. London: Penguin.

Hindess, Barry. 2004. "Liberalism - what's in a name?" In *Global Governmentality: Governing International Spaces*, edited by W. Larner and W. Walters. London: Routledge.

Hsu, S. S., and M. B. Sheridan. 2009. "Anti-Drug Effort at Border is Readied"; *The Washington Post* (March 22, 2009); available at: http://www.washingtonpost.com/wp-dyn/content/article/2009/03/21/AR2009032102247.html (accessed 02/08/2010).

Justice, U.S. Department of. 2009. "Prisoners in 2008"; *Bureau of Justice Statistics Bulletin*; available at: http://bjs.ojp.usdoj.gov/index.cfm?ty=pbdetail&iid=1764 (accessed 04/01/2010).

Kan, Paul R. 2009. *Drugs and Contemporary Warfare*. Washington, D.C.: Potomac Books.

Kienscherf, Markus. 2010. "Plugging Cultural Knowledge into the U.S. Military Machine: The Neo-Orientalist Logic of Counterinsurgency." *Topia - Canadian Journal of Cultural Studies* (23-24):121-143.

Kilcullen, David J. 2005. "Countering global insurgency." *Journal of Strategic Studies* 28 (4):597-617.

————. 2009. *The Accidental Guerrilla: Fighting Small Wars in the Midst of a Big One*. Oxford: Oxford University Press.

Lahav, Gallya. 2008. "Mobility and Border Security: The U.S. Aviation System, the State, and the Rise of Public-Private Partnerships." In *Politics at the Airport*, edited by M. B. Salter. Minneapolis: University of Minnesota Press.

Long, Austin. 2006. *On "Other War": Lessons from Five Decades of RAND Counterinsurgency Research*. Santa Monica, CA: RAND Corporation.

Lyon, David. 2008. "Filtering Flows, Friends, and Foes." In *Politics at the Airport*, edited by M. B. Salter. Minneapolis: University of Minnesota Press.

Marenko, Tamara. 2002. "Crime, Terror and the Central Asian Drug Trade"; *Asia Quarterly* (3 (Summer 2002)); available at: http://www.asiaquarterly.com/content/view/121/40/ (accessed 4 June 2010).

Marshall, J. 1987. "Drugs and United States Foreign Policy." In *Dealing with Drugs*, edited by R. Hamowy. Lexington, Mass.: D. C. Heath and Co.

Morales, W. Q. 1989. "The war on drugs: a new US national security doctrine?" *Third World Quarterly* 11 (3):147-169.

Nixon, R. M. 1969. "Text of Nixon message on plan to attack drugs abuse." In *Congressional Quarterly Almanac*. Washington D.C.: CQ Press.

Parenti, Christian. 1999. *Lockdown America: Police and Prisons in the Age of Crisis*. London: Verso.

Salter, Mark B. 2005. "At the threshold of security: a theory of international borders." In *Global Surveillance and Policing: Borders, Security, Identity*, edited by E. Zureik and M. B. Salter. Portland, Oregon: Willan Publishing.

———. 2008a. "Introduction: Airport Assemblage." In *Politics at the Airport*, edited by M. B. Salter. Minneapolis: University of Minnesota Press.

———. 2008b. "The Global Aiport: Managing Space, Speed, and Security." In *Politics at the Airport*, edited by M. B. Salter. Minneapolis: University of Minnesota Press.

Sparke, M. B. 2006. "A Neoliberal Nexus: Economy, Security and the Biopolitics of Citizenship on the Border." *Political Geography* 25 (2):151-180.

Ucko, David H. 2009. *The New Counterinsurgency Era: Transforming the U.S. Military for Modern Wars*. Washington D.C.: Georgetown University Press.

USJFC. 2008. "The Joint Operating Environment 2008: Challenges and Implications for the Future Joint Forces"; available at: http://www.jfcom.mil/newslink/storyarchive/2008/JOE2008.pdf (accessed 02/08/2010).

Wacquant, L. 2001. "Deadly symbiosis: when ghetto and prison meet and mesh." *Punishment and Society* 3 (1):95-134.

Weizman, Eyal. 2007. *Hollow land: Israel's architecture of occupation*. London: Verso.

Zureik, E., and M. B. Salter. 2005. "Global surveillance and policing: borders, security, identity - Introduction." In *Global Surveillance and Policing: Borders, Security, Identity*, edited by E. Zureik and M. B. Salter. Portland, Oregon: Willan Publishing.

A new collection, from
CAROLINA ACADEMIC PRESS ...

Protest and Punishment:
The Repression of Resistance in the Era of Neoliberal Globalization

Edited by: Jeff Shantz

> " In the wake of a global economic crisis, resistance to neoliberalism has become ever more important while state repression has become increasingly severe. Shantz's collection is thus a welcome addition to this debate. "
>
> -Tom Malleson, Editor of *Whose Streets? The Toronto G20 and the Challenges of Summit Protest*

Seattle (1999), Quebec City (2001), Genoa (2001), Miami (2003), London (2009), Toronto (2010)
Neo-liberal states' immigration policies & migrant revolt; Black Bloc tactics; Martial law in Canada; Indigenous Resistance; COINTELPRO to the "war on terror"; initial notes on Occupy & much more...

These histories, these many running street battles between demonstrators and police, are here examined in detail for their lessons.

294 pp • paper •
ISBN: 978-1-61163-088-6
• LCCN 2011052597

http://jeffshantz.ca/PnP

Contesting the "Justice Campus": Abolitionist Resistance to Liberal Carceral Expansion

JUDAH SCHEPT,
EASTERN KENTUCKY UNIVERSITY

INTRODUCTION:
SCENES OF DISJUNCTURE

I am sitting in the audience in a meeting room at the public library in the vibrant downtown center of Springfield, a Midwestern small city home to a large university.[1] I am one of perhaps 45 community residents who have gathered to hear current and campaigning county politicians speak about the local criminal justice system and recently announced plans for its expansion. Downtown Springfield is full of independent restaurants, cafes, boutiques, independent book and music stores, and a food cooperative, all pointing to the community's politically progressive identity. Indeed, the elderly man about to speak at the podium in the meeting room is a long-time Democratic county politician and Quaker peace activist, who also frequently criticizes mass incarceration. As this man, Reuben Davison, began to speak to the public, he offered a line that I had heard him say in previous meetings and that I would come to hear him say several more times:

"The shame of this country in the 18th century was slavery. The shame of this county in the 19th century was Jim Crow. The shame of this country in the 20th and 21st centuries is the prison industrial complex."

---

[1] The author would like to thank Phil Parnell, Stephanie Kane, Khalil Muhammad, Hal Pepinsky and Kip Schlegel for their invaluable criticism and advice on the larger ethnography of which is this essay is a part. In addition, the author wishes to thank Tyler Wall for his helpful comments on this essay.

On this and future evenings, Davison followed his oratory locating mass incarceration as part of a historical trajectory of racist institutions with a seemingly incongruous second point. Following his condemnation of the prison industrial complex, Davison would invariably offer an emphatic and passionate embrace of his and other county leaders' proposal to build a "justice campus," an 85 acre complex of new carceral facilities that would exponentially expand the county's ability to incarcerate adults and youth. Advocates of the justice campus imagined its constitutive institutions—a large new county jail, a juvenile facility, and a work release center—to be extensions of the community's progressive politics, model facilities that operated outside of history and dislocated from contemporary penal politics. Indeed, at the forum in the library and at many other community meetings I attended in Springfield, advocates of expansion articulated their vision of the campus through discourses of rehabilitation, education, therapeutic justice and human rights. That is, the discourse supporting massive carceral expansion was bereft of any invocation of punishment.

It was the disjuncture between Davison's and many others' critical analysis of mass incarceration and their unabashed endorsement of local carceral expansion that brought me to the meeting and the ethnography of which it was a part. After more than a year as a community organizer with Decarcerate Lincoln County (DLC), a local organization challenging the justice campus, I formally began ethnographic study of the discourse and politics of carceral expansion and resistance to it. I spent the next two years immersed in the issues, conducting interviews and attending community meetings with county politicians, civic leaders, corrections officials, private consultants, social workers, and community activists. As someone who had been involved for many years prior in prison activism that focused on the punitive state, I was consistently struck by the incongruence of community leaders' condemnation of mass incarceration and advocacy for a massive, if benevolent, justice campus.

In this essay, it is this disjuncture—the embrace of liberal carcerality and the rejection of the carceral state and nation—that forms my starting point of examination and a point of departure for the central exploration of these pages: resistance to liberal carceral expansion. I draw on interviews and participant observation to illustrate the diverse ways in which community activists intervened in the narrative of carceral expansion.[2] I try to convey my observations through both "thick

---

[2] All place, personal, and organizational names are pseudonyms.

description" (Geertz 1973) and through the critically important project of locating analysis of the "local" amidst the moving and implicating currents of mass incarceration and the broader political-economic and cultural flows of which it is a part (Appadurai 1996; Clifford and Marcus 1986; Gupta and Ferguson 1997; Smith 2001).

At times, local officials in favor of the campus were able to co-opt activists' interventions and fold them back into the dominant narrative of the justice campus. Other times, however, activists succeeded in disrupting the dominant articulation of local carcerality. In exploring both abolitionist community organizing as well as covert and anonymous acts of property destruction targeting the machinery of expansion, this article offers ethnographic explorations of the ways in which communities contest some of the more insidious logics of carceral expansion.

TRANS-LOCAL CARCERALITY

Towards the end of 2007, the county found itself under threat of a lawsuit because of conditions at the jail due to overcrowding. Built in 1986 to house 126 inmates and double bunked in 2006, the jail held well over 300 prisoners by the end 2007 and the beginning of 2008. The county hired Project Administration Results, Inc. (PARI), a private firm specializing in corrections construction, to research and plan a "justice campus." The complex would sit on an 85 acre lot purchased by the county in 2002, and would include a new jail with double the capacity of the current one (between 400 and 500 beds), a new 72 bed juvenile facility, a 100 bed work release center, and various new offices for criminal justice professionals. Built into the proposal and the architectural rendering of the campus was the ability for each facility to double in size. The official price tag of the facility was estimated to be between $50 and $75 million dollars.

Mapped onto the decrepit 85 acre site of the proposed justice campus is a larger story that provides important historical-political context. The 85 acres, known colloquially as "the old TDA site," once housed a multinational manufacturing company that was, for decades during the middle of the 20th century, the largest employer in the county. The company, which I'll call Technology Development of America, shed almost 10,000 local jobs en route to ultimately departing Springfield for Mexico at the end of the 1990s. Thus, the concept of the justice campus would not have been possible without a particular historical trajectory, one that should sound familiar to those with some knowledge of the growth of mass incarceration. It is a story of the departure of capital and industry; of shady partnerships between private capital and politics; and of incarceration as the catchall—and, crucially, the inevitable—solution to problems raised by capital's departure.[3]

Of course, a county seeking to expand exponentially its ability to incarcerate is not a new story. Indeed, since the late 1990s, scholars, journalists, and activists have used the term *prison industrial complex* (PIC) to refer to the growth in size, scope and centrality of the correctional institution, as well as its interdependency with private economic interests. Scholarship has profiled the rise of the prison industrial complex through narratives that privilege political economy, in particular neoliberal globalization (Gilmore 2007; Hallett 2006), conservative cultural values and political ideologies (Garland 2001), punitive public policy (Currie 1998; Mauer 2000), and various combinations thereof (Austin & Irwin 2001; Donziger, [Ed.] 1996). Included in these and other analyses of mass incarceration are poignant observations of the racialized nature of mass incarceration, with scholars noting the historical criminalization of blackness (Muhammad, 2010), the contemporary disproportionate imprisonment of people of color (Gilmore 2007; James [Ed.] 2007, 2002; Loury 2008), and the collateral consequences of such racialized incarceration (Clear 2007; Mauer & Chesney-Lind 2002), including the extension of Jim Crow discrimination through incarceration (Alexander 2009).

What makes this story seemingly distinct is the overwhelming presence of people like Reuben Davison at the forefront of advocacy for the justice campus. That is, no one with whom I spoke disputed the findings, explanations and critiques of the above scholars. Often, advocates of the justice campus offered unprompted indictments of mass incarceration. In their words, the justice campus would embody and express the distinct nature of local progressive politics, eschewing punishment for rehabilitation and education, and in the process, reducing recidivism, healing drug addiction, and providing much needed edu-

---

[3] Readers interested in a more comprehensive account of the transnational movement of capital and the loss of jobs should see Jefferson Cowie's (1999) *Capital Moves*.

cation. Indeed, in the very name "justice campus", officials mapped the bucolic and collegiate identity of the town onto their proposal for the most drastic expansion of carceral control in county history. But in officials' refusal—or inability—to consider reducing community reliance on incarceration and in the myriad ways in which they marginalized important voices, local activists found critical entries into contesting the campus.

DEFINING RESISTANCE

Describing the contestation of carceral expansion in this essay as "resistance" raises some challenges, both theoretical and empirical, because of the specific cultural-political context of my research site. Some respondents who *advocated* for carceral expansion identified that work as resisting mass incarceration. In the context of Lincoln County carceral politics, resistance is a contested term, devoid of essential meaning and utilized within diverse political contexts. This raises complicated questions. What is resistance and how does one observe it in the field? What distinguishes resistance from other political activity? Beyond these definitional issues the researcher faces larger, reflexive issues. Am I engaging in and perpetuating a "theoretical hegemony of resistance" (Brown 1996, 279) within ethnographic scholarship, undermining the analytical utility of the concept and, in Brown's (1996, 730) snarky but poignant words, "strongly skewing the project of cultural anthropology in the direction inspired by the work of Foucault: culture as prison, culture as insane asylum, culture as 'hegemonic domination of the [insert Other of choice]'"?

Moreover, as raised by Brown (1996) and others (Fletcher 2007), scholarship has increasingly turned toward "everyday acts" of resistance (Abu Lughod 1990; Scott 1990; 1985) and celebratory moments of transgression (Ferrell, Hayward and Young 2008; Ferrell 2007; Hall and Winlow 2007). Some scholarship has sought to warn against such a trend, noting, for example, that a consequence of the postmodern attention to decentralized and individualistic acts of resistance, at the expense of a focus on collective struggles and social movements, can be the disabling of a transformative politics (Handler 1993).

Crucially, some scholars, such as Jeff Ferrell, identify the moments observed in ethnographic study of resistance and transgression as constitutive of larger, coordinated movements. In an article responding to criticism of cultural criminology's focus on such moments, Ferrell (2007, 94) rhetorically asks, "Can phenomena like "subversive symbol inversion' and "creative recoding' actually be found, and more importantly, found to constitute a significant opposition to capitalism's suffocations?"

Of course, this essay does not resolve these tensions (and does not attempt to). Ultimately, in the definition of resistance by which I abide—resistance seeks radical changes in power relations (McCann 2006)—I am able to acknowledge the diversity that exists in resistant articulations. In this standpoint, I do, in a way, take sides within the debates on resistance. I believe, contrary to Brown (1996), that resistance remains a crucial analytic. Indeed, against his criticism of the scholarly hegemony of resistance, I rather proudly align myself as attempting to further instantiate that particular hegemonic articulation.

Resistance to the carceral state—and, crucially, resistance to the diverse, decentralized, and distinctive articulations of the carceral state, such as municipal jail expansion—is of paramount importance both to scholars of resistance and to other readers interested and engaged in activism and community organizing. The nature of local resistance to the justice campus is nothing short of an attempt at social change through a radical destabilization of habitus (Schaeffer 2004, 123). Although DLC can be understood as engaging in a series of specific campaigns, some of which were modest in their demands and reformist in their orientations, there was an unmistakable and often explicit attempt to change the very dispositions with which local officials and others viewed such issues and concepts heavy with hegemonic inscription as crime, safety, police, and, of course, incarceration. In this way, McCann's definition of resistance applies well to the work of DMC and others in their contestations over carceral expansion, to which I now turn.

RESISTING LIBERAL CARCERALITY:
DECARCERATE LINCOLN COUNTY

Decarcerate Lincoln County (DLC) formed in the summer of 2008 after several months of conversations among a growing group of concerned residents. Beginning in the early spring of that year, individuals met with growing regularity to discuss interventions into the justice campus conversation in the community. The initial conversations among four activists, including myself, quickly became larger meetings. In May of 2008, the small group organized a day of popular education about the prison industrial complex and the justice campus that drew over 70 participants, including several politicians and judges.

DLC included people with varying experiences of community organizing and activism and with different political orientations. Several people involved with DLC were concurrently engaged in eco-defense work against Interstate 69, the so-called NAFTA superhighway. To an extent, some of these activists attended DLC meetings to gain a better understanding of linkages between anti-jail and anti-globalization work. One DLC activist, Michaela Davis, astutely noted to me that incarceration is the common denominator linking struggles; as a locus of repression and control, prison is the site where seemingly disparate struggles converge.

Other people involved with DLC had longer histories of prison activism, most notably with Critical Resistance (CR), a national organization dedicated to the abolition of the prison industrial complex.[4] The connection to CR would prove important for a number of reasons. The organization at times served as a conduit for DLC's articulation of the justice campus as one site among many in the diverse manifestations of the prison industrial complex. CR also fostered DLC's understanding of itself as part of a broader, even transnational, network of resistance. Moreover, CR's explicitly abolitionist framework would prove to be invaluable for DLC's own identity formation and for their development of a local alternative framework through which to criticize the justice campus and its accompanying "progressive" discourses.

DLC's resistance focused on stopping the construction and implementation of the justice campus. But that goal was set in a broader discursive context of trying to intervene in and disrupt the liberal carceral narrative that identified a benevolent and curative justice campus as a human rights solution to the human rights problem of overcrowding at the current jail. This broader context would prove crucial for DLC to remain an active voice

---

[4] See http://www.criticalresistance.org

in community discussions of social control, as the eventual defeat of the justice campus proposal simply meant that new initiatives for expansion surfaced. DLC's identification with abolitionist principles provided a consistent framework for offering indictments of liberal attempts to shape incarceration to fit the political context of the community.

Yet staking their claim in abolition also brought with it various internal and external challenges, including the negotiation within the group of different orientations to radical politics, the constant struggle to prioritize the voices and needs of the people most affected by incarceration, and the rather uncharted territory of organizing against incarceration when it's advocates were primarily members of the community's liberal and progressive establishment.

Indeed, in officials' embrace of therapeutic justice and rehabilitation and active critique of punishment, they presented a formidable challenge to organizers against jail expansion. Rather than relying on resistant discourses that critiqued state power and punishment, organizers had to articulate a coherent critique of local, benevolent carcerality.

Moreover, organizers encountered discursive and strategic challenges when county officials spoke not only of rehabilitation and human rights, but also of debate, consensus, and public opinion. Thus, community organizers faced campaigns for carceral expansion that relied on liberal discourses of incarceration to envision institutions and rhetoric of democratic process and community consensus to legitimate them.

As such, two larger themes characterized the resistant articulations of county activists. The first and most explicit was the attempt by activists to disrupt the liberal carceral narrative of county leaders. Activists attempted to point to the ways in which decarceration—the overall reduction of the county's reliance on incarceration—provided long term, sustainable solutions to the problems of the county. That is, activists pointed to mass incarceration as the root problem through which other problems manifested.

The second theme of resistor discourse was the contestation of county processes of knowledge production and political decision-making. Activists frequently questioned the formation and privileging of knowledge and the methods by which county officials discussed issues and formed policy. In addition to offering criticisms of these phenomena at county events, activists attempted to embody the structures of decision-making and knowledge production that they wished to see more broadly. For example, internal DLC meetings utilized consensus decision-making and followed a number of guidelines to facilitate non-hierarchical and anti-oppression processes. DLC utilized similar models at larger, community forums that the group organized, including orchestrating the geography of the meeting room to reflect egalitarian principles. In contrast to county-organized meetings where there was always some demarcation between officials and the public, DLC intentionally constructed circles at most meetings.[5]

DISRUPTING DOXA:
FROM CARCERAL NATURALIZATION
TO ABOLITIONIST AWARENESS

One way to understand the support for the justice campus in Lincoln County is through the idea that carcerality—the logic and practice of physical and coercive control—operates at the level of habitus. That is, the hegemony of mass incarceration inscribes into individual and organizational bodies a set of dispositions and practices that operate at the level of common sense, such that critics of incarceration still turn to forms of carcerality (the justice campus) to address problems of carcerality (jail overcrowding).

Pierre Bourdieu's (1977; 1990; 1991; 2005) work on the concept of habitus is instructive. Bourdieu notes that within habitus exist different dispositions, including *orthodoxy* and *doxa*. Bourdieu distinguishes the two by noting that doxa refers to the self-evidentiary appearance of the social world; in contrast to orthodox or heterodox beliefs that realize different or antagonistic belief structures, doxa occurs when there is unquestioned (and unquestionable) adherence to a "world of tradition experienced as a "natural world' and taken for granted" (1977, 164).

Local carcerality operated as both orthodoxy and doxa in Springfield. Officials in favor of the justice campus understood that they had choices when it came to planning for the future of

---

[5] On utilizing Circles for community planning, see Ball, Caldwell and Pranis (2010)

incarceration and youth detention. In their informed and at times passionate denouncements of mass incarceration and simultaneous articulation of local carcerality, officials demonstrated their understanding of the diverse iterations of and beliefs about institutions. But this orthodoxy existed within a bounded universe of discourse in the community; carcerality, the control and detention embodied in not only the justice campus but also subsequent proposals and "alternatives", made certain perspectives, such as abolitionist change, undiscussable. If one can understand culture as "the very material of…daily lives, the bricks and mortar of…most commonplace understandings" (Willis 1979, 184-5), then within the context of the community the *discursive* bricks and mortar that constructed and maintained local cultural understandings of carcerality also served to structure and limit the conversations about criminal justice, predicating any discussion of reform on the *physical* bricks and mortar of institutions.[6]

In this section I examine DLC's significant interventions into the dominant county narrative, bringing the "undiscussable into discussion" and, for certain periods of time, enacting counter-hegemonic understandings of key issues. Critical interventions into the carceral discourse occurred through three thematic means: 1) direct challenges to benevolent carcerality, 2) direct challenges to the structure of meetings and the production of knowledge, and 3) the reframing of key issues that successfully inscribed counter-hegemonic understanding into the discourse, if only temporarily. In DLC's work to bring abolition into discussion, the group contributed to what Bourdieu sees as the beginning of political consciousness (Bourdieu 1977, 170).

DIRECT CHALLENGES: CONFRONTING LIBERAL CARCERALITY

In the fall of 2008, the local criminal justice advisory body, the Lincoln County Criminal Justice Coordinating Board (LC-CJCB), organized four public meetings whose official purpose was to obtain public input. The first three meetings focused on the three major constitutive parts of the justice campus—the juvenile facility, the work release center, and the jail—and the fourth examined the official master plan for the site. The LC-CJCB was comprised of officials who were active supporters of

---

[6] See Sloop (1996) for important work on cultural and discursive constructs of prison

the campus and all four meetings featured the county's consultant for the campus, Project Administration Results, Inc. The spatial privilege afforded to officials and experts, and their location at the beginning of meeting agendas in order to present material and frame subsequent discussions, inevitably resulted in their ability to consistently restate their positions and respond to public criticism in ways that often reframed resistant articulations into endorsements of expansion. Activists and other community residents who attended the meetings reported to me that they were "farcical" and "scripted". One disaffected county politician who was a one-time outspoken proponent of the justice campus told me that the four meetings were "token attempts to 'checklist' public process."

Interestingly, despite the scripted nature of the meetings and their imposing and formal spatial arrangements, some of Decarcerate Lincoln County's more powerful interventions occurred during public comment at the meetings. In these moments, activists often utilized direct and personal stories to explicitly criticize the county's perspective. In leveling devastating critiques through narrative accounts, activists no doubt found meaning in sharing their personal stories but also expressed an epistemological challenge to what the group saw as a depersonalized and disembodied official narrative.

At the third LCCJCB meeting about the justice campus, which focused on the jail, DLC member Emily Collins mapped a genealogy of alcoholism and incarceration in her family to illustrate the linkages between jail, poverty, and addiction:

> My name is Emily Collins and I'm a member of a group called DLC. I joined that group for a number of reasons. My family has a long history of generational recidivism. My great-grandfather was an alcoholic, but a wealthy alcoholic, so he spent very little time in jail. My grandfather, his son, was a middle-class alcoholic and spent increasingly more time in jail. My uncles, his sons, were alcoholics and drug addicts but they were very poor so they spent years and years in jail. My cousins and brothers are already spending time in jail. I've witnessed firsthand that the fastest way to ensure that somebody is going to spend time in jail is to send them there in the first place or send their parents to jail. And I've seen this happen. It seems like the longer the problem goes down the generational line without somebody treating it, the younger it starts in the next generation. I've noticed that jail doesn't work yet other programs are not as heavily funded as jails are...you don't sentence people to treatment you sentence them to jail time. That doesn't work. I've no-

ticed first hand it's not effective. And the reason I've joined this group that is trying to stop this jail from happening is that I strongly believe in one of the demands that we must treat drug addiction not criminalize it. I'm not talking about simply reducing recidivism, but about not sending sick people to jail in the first place.

Collins's personal and passionate account of generational addiction and incarceration posited important arguments about the criminalization of addiction and the targeting of the poor.[7] Crucially, she shaped her account not only to share this important story, but also to wield it politically against the prevailing narrative that offered the justice campus as precisely the place where people like her family members could be treated. In what seemed to be anticipation of that response from the panel, Collins closed her statements by saying that treating addiction must mean not sending people to jail in the first place.

Most advocates of the justice campus pointed to poverty's overwhelming role in incarceration through softly pathologizing poor people, a construction of poverty that had the added bonus of granting legitimacy to the curative and benevolent facility they imagined as having a role in poor people's rehabilitation.[8] In contrast, DLC activists like Emily Collins worked hard to problematize normative definitions of crime, de-link criminality from poverty, push for non-institutional and non-punitive ways to approach social problems, and demonstrated the targeting of poor people by the criminal justice system. In this latter effort, DLC co-founder Michaela Davis pointed out the problematic structure of probation fees during the same meeting:

> Currently, the fees of people who are on probation pay the salaries of probation officers. This creates a perverse incentive structure so that probation officers need to maintain high amounts of people on probation in order to be sure their salaries are paid. I think it's broadly recognized that this is a bad incentive structure, but there's no other funding that is coming through, and if we can't provide the funding to change that kind of incentive structure I'm curious how we will have the funding available after we build a larger jail. I think changing that probation funding is one of those small institutional steps that we could take to change the causes of overcrowding. I think there are lots of other ones.

---

[7] See Donziger, (Ed.) (1996), Irwin (1992), Mauer (2006), and Reiman (2000), for further discussion of the relationships between poverty, the war on drugs, and incarceration.

[8] Muhammad (2010) has called this the writing of crime into class.

In this statement, Michaela Davis revealed an insidious and problematic arrangement within the system: probationer fees funded the probation department's personnel costs. As Davis pointed out, this incentivized systemic growth.[9] She positioned her comments to subvert the very foundation on which the justice campus was predicated: to accommodate the size of the system. Davis pointed out to the panel how the system's structure produced the problems that required expansion. In proposing real, practical, and small steps to shrink the system and thus alleviate those problems, Davis artfully framed an abolitionist analysis to fit the reformist context of the meeting.

DIRECT CHALLENGES: PROBLEMATIZING PROCESS

In addition to direct challenges to the articulation of liberal carcerality, DLC members also confronted the knowledge production and political processes that constructed and insulated the dominant narrative of expansion. DLC challenged the dominant subjectivity of meeting spaces and the committed epistemologies of practitioners and consultants during public meetings. At meetings hosted by DLC, the group prioritized the voices of counter-experts: the people and families most affected by carceral policies.

DLC's challenge to the epistemologies and politics of the justice campus was an important ideological contestation of the meaning of local carcerality. John Thompson's (1986) study of ideology, in particular his claim that "to study ideology is to study the ways in which meaning (signification) serves to sustain relations of domination" (131), provides important theoretical context for understanding DLC's ardent focus on challenging official process. Thompson writes that,

> What may have seemed like a sphere of effective *consensus* must in many cases be seen as a realm of actual or potential *conflict*. Hence the meaning of what is said…is infused with forms of power; different individuals or groups have a differential capacity to *make a meaning stick* (Thompson 1986, 132).[10]

---

[9] Shelden (2010, p. 58) notes that this same arrangement defined jails from their beginnings. He writes, "It was ironic that the financing of local jails depended on fees paid to jailers by those confined there when the majority of jail prisoners were drawn from the poorest classes." Summarizing McConville (1995), he continues, "Phrased another way, fees were extracted "from misery.""

INVISIBILITY

Decarcerate Lincoln County had an organizational priority of integrating the people most affected by criminal justice policies into their campaigns. The group was highly concerned about the absence of marginalized county residents from the consultant's reports and during official meetings. In criticizing the processes of the justice campus, activists poignantly positioned the hiring of outside consultants against the exclusion of the local community.

Although the Lincoln County Criminal Justice Coordinate Board facilitated the justice campus process with the cooperation of a number of different individuals and agencies, DLC focused much of their criticism on the county's consultant, PARI. This made sense on both emotional and political grounds, with a prison and jail construction firm from outside of the community being a rather easy target for activists' derision. While criticizing PARI in a public meeting served the important purpose of intervening in a discourse that suggested the justice campus was the product of community consensus, it was not necessarily the best strategic choice. As the history of county carcerality demonstrated, consultants came and went but the county habitus that made the justice campus possible stayed. Had DLC challenged the local actors and local logics that made the hiring of PARI not only possible, but also inevitable, there may have been a more effective destabilization of the habitus.

At the LCCJCB meeting about the juvenile facility, DLC member Helen Bishop, who later would run for city council, challenged the panel:

> I don't know why we have a company here that makes money from building these facilities. Why don't we have people who build YM-CAs and youth centers at the table too, different perspectives from people who don't benefit from building [jails]? Why don't we have youth who have been through the system, who can present the challenges that they had? I know you guys said you've been working on this for years, but whom are you including in the conversation? How can we change this conversation to include everybody? Are you guys just having these meetings as a write-off, "OK, we've talked to the public now let's go build a facility'?

---

[10] See Paley (2004) for important ethnographic scholarship examining the ideological uses of democratic discourse by Chilean officials to limit the abilities of community groups to participate in political processes.

Helen Bishop's testimony offered important analysis of the local conflict. In her suggestion that PARI shouldn't be at the meetings and instead that other companies who build recreational facilities should be present, she offered a powerful rhetorical move that destabilized the popular narrative that jails and detention had to serve as the institutional homes for programs. Moreover, Bishop pushed the panel on who they considered to be an important part of the process and who was and should have been included in the conversation.

At the third LCCJCB meeting focused on the jail, DLC member Ruth Laurel addressed PARI founder and CEO Richard Kemp directly:

> I heard you speaking a lot tonight about what "we" have told you that we want. You've said over and over "you want this" and "you want that" but I and a lot of people that I know have not talked to you and have not had an opportunity to have our interests known and it really bothers me to have someone tell me what I want when they have not talked to me. So that goes for a lot of people in Springfield and a lot of the people that those people know. It's not clear to me who in the community—regular citizens—has been a part of that process.

Ruth Laurel pointed out that the "you" to whom PARI referred constituted a narrow segment of the local population, largely comprised of officials, civic leaders, and criminal justice professionals. Thus, the "consensus" to which Kemp had referred existed among institutionally positioned participants in the county criminal justice establishment. Themes that emerged from Kemp's conversations with people were of a limited nature by design, and certainly did not reflect—at least not necessarily so—the wishes or analyses of the larger community.

In a similar comment, Dave Santiago questioned the very premise that PARI should be having conversations with anyone, regardless of how limited or inclusive they might have been:

> I don't think it's appropriate either that when someone [comments to the panel] "we want to have dialogue with all these different kinds of people' then the response is "well, the PARI corporate representative who profits off of prisons and jails has talked to those people, so you know, rest easy." *We* need to talk to those people; we don't need to talk to [Richard Kemp]. He shouldn't even be in the room until we, as a community, have decided what we want.

The county commissioners, the county's executive body, hired PARI. In the integral role PARI played in the official justice campus public meetings, it is clear that officials saw the company as part of the decision-making of the community. For Dave Santiago and other DLC activists, the presence of consultants delegitimized any claim by the county to objectivity. Moreover, the usage of consultants who profited off of jail expansion aided the attempts by DLC to locate county carcerality as part of mass incarceration.

One final example provides an especially poignant illustration of the different priorities between officials and activists regarding the visibility of people most affected by incarceration. DLC member Haley Ralston spoke to the panel at the third MCCJCC meeting, following Ruth Laurel. She was speaking about the ways in which the jail acted as a debtor's prison when she mentioned, almost offhand, that people most affected by jail policies were not part of the process. Tom Grady, a local attorney and one of two citizen appointees to the LCCJCB, then interrupted to ask her to clarify what she meant:

> *Tom Grady:* And by that do you mean the inmates or the people who get arrested, or…what do you mean by the people most affected?
>
> *Haley Ralston:* Yes and yes and the people on probation and the people who deal with day reporting and the people who have families who deal with those things and who are so obviously underrepresented in these forums that the focus of the questions about who knows anything about jail is phrased as a question of who has been on a tour. That's a problem for me. "Cause that really speaks to the fact that we aren't representative of the voices of the people who are intended to be affected by the systems you all are creating.

Haley Ralston astutely observed the implicit assumptions of the meeting's organizers: that meeting attendees would only know the jail through tours, as opposed to having been incarcerated or having a family member incarcerated. In their constructions of who has access to community meetings, who wants to attend, and who should care, officials excluded those people most affected by criminal justice policies. Moreover, in their exclusion, officials also rendered to the margins other ways of experiencing jail, including as a prisoner or as a loved one. In their construction of who should be and was in the room for the discussion of the jail, the only way one could know the jail was through being a practitioner, a volunteer, or by going on a tour.[11]

VISIBILITY AND EPISTEMOLOGY: THE FREE VOICES PROJECT

DLC employed different means to attempt to model the kind of visibility and accountability that the group claimed was lacking from official processes. This commitment took on various forms, including holding meetings in locations and at times more convenient to certain populations, such as family members of people incarcerated at the county jail; using consensus processes and horizontal decision-making, an attempt to embody a non-hierarchical structure;[12] and conducting community canvassing to organize people to attend community meetings. While the group had inconsistent successes with these attempts, the group did formalize some of these processual concerns into a formal campaign: The Free Voices Project.

The Free Voices Project began early in DLC's life, during the summer of 2008. The group modeled the Free Voices Project on a composite of other projects, including storytelling projects in various cities and the work of other incarceration-related organizations that utilized media to express the narratives of prisoners and their families. Out of a series of meetings focused on developing the project, DLC identified the following goals:

> 1. *Content:* Creating a community counter-narrative of the prison industrial complex in Springfield through a process that prioritizes people's experiences, articulates those experiences in peo-

---

[11]But framing attainment of knowledge of a jail through participation in a tour has other implications as well. Whereas some noted sociologists (Wacquant, 2002) have embraced, and even advocated for, the carceral tour as an important tool of research and education, others have been critical of the tour's ability, even purpose, to enact specific knowledge that both protects and validates institutional practices (Goffman, 1961; Piche and Walby, 2010). In the present study, it appeared that the tour had a more complicated purpose. Given the mission of the panel to promote the construction of a new justice campus, it seems likely that the tour, in their minds at least, would have advanced that goal, likely demonstrating the various problems with institutional capacity and overcrowding. Thus, the tour would have transparently depicted the problems with the jail while also being wielded as a tool to promote institutional expansion.

[12]David Graeber (2007) has made the point that these practices are perhaps best described by the analytic term "democracy."

ple's own words, and facilitates connections between folks traditionally separated by race and class barriers.

2. ***Process:*** Pursuing these goals through an organizing process that empowers participants, doesn't replicate traditional, hierarchical power dynamics, and which undermines problematic representations of people's voices and experiences.

3. ***Political:*** Remaining committed to a larger political vision that opposes jail construction, challenges problematic figures in the criminal justice system, promotes community decarceration, and advocates for alternative models of conflict resolution.

DLC members active in the Free Voices Project primarily attended the twice-a-week all-cell-block visiting hours at the jail. There, family members would gather in an alley on the west side of the building to sign in and then wait, sometime for many hours, for the cell block of their loved one to be called for visitation. This spatial and temporal liminality was to become a contested state in years to come. While waiting in the alley certainly placed a burden on families, it also created important ties and was a part of the process for families in order to see their loved ones in person. After the $75 million dollar PARI proposal was defeated, the jail commander offered his own proposal to renovate the current jail for just under one million dollars. Included in the renovations was the complete shift from in-person visitation to video-conferencing.

The time in the alley proved conducive to the Free Voices Project. DLC members would arrive and spend hours talking with people waiting to visit. At various times, DLC members administered surveys and conducted in-depth interviews, using audio recorders when possible and when people consented. The time spent with visitors also served to complicate DLC's politics. Frequently, people in the alley cited police practices, arbitrary probation policies, and drug and alcohol problems, including the absence of diverse programming, as their central concerns. While DLC kept their overall focus on challenging jail expansion and promoting decarceration, conversations in the alley ultimately diversified DLC's focus. By recording visitors' testimonies, the group could relay their perspectives directly to people in power, challenging both official content and epistemology. In one especially powerful recording, two DLC members spoke with people in the alley about the proposed changes to visitation. A local community radio station gave DLC digital audio recorders and then broadcast the edited recording. DLC members also went to county commissioner meetings and read excerpts of the testimonies to the commissioners.

RADICAL REFRAMING:
FROM CARCERAL EXPANSION TO COMMUNITY SAFETY

In addition to intervening in liberal carcerality and epistemology and attempting to model alternatives through the Free Voices Project, DLC reframed key concepts embedded in discourses of social control as another activist tactic to bring into discussion the previously undiscussable. In forcing the community, including politicians, to reflect on what brought about individual and community safety, DLC successfully disrupted a rather narrow linear narrative that connected safety to a robust, if benevolent, criminal justice system.

In moving from the direct confrontation I profiled in the previous sections to this section's focus on DLC's counter-hegemonic articulation of key concepts, I see a mapping out of the distinction that Laclau and Mouffe (1985, 189) call the "strategy of opposition" versus the "strategy of construction of a new order." The authors write that,

> In the case of the first, the element of negation of a certain social or political order predominates, but this element of negativity is not accompanied by any real attempt to establish different nodal points from which a process of different and positive reconstruction of the social fabric could be instituted—and as a result the strategy is condemned to marginality...In the case of the strategy of construction of a new order, in contrast, the element of social positivity predominates, but this very fact creates an unstable balance and a constant tension with the subversive logic of democracy.

DLC's first official event in the late spring of 2008 brought together over 70 people, including older activists from a local group providing jail programming, young anarchists involved in eco-defense work, local non-profit leaders, and several politicians and criminal justice officials. DLC framed the day as popular education about the prison industrial complex and the local justice campus. Not coincidentally, the county primary elections were just days later, and the group had compiled a list of candidate perspectives on the issues of carceral expansion. Sitting in chairs and on the floor in the backroom of a local independent and radical book store, DLC organizers led attendees through several different exercises designed to both educate about local and national histories of incarceration and foster an open but radically situated discussion, one not confined by official discourses but, instead, encouraging of realms of possibilities beyond the immediately practical.

One of the day's first events was a short exercise that I facilitated. The question that DLC posed to attendees was "What Makes Our Community, and we as Individuals, Safe?" The response was rapid and enthusiastic, with comments ranging from liberal concerns of equality to radical challenges to liberal categories. Below is a partial list of what was said:

> Knowing neighbors; keeping police out of my neighborhood; food access; green spaces; places to sleep; good paying jobs; social and economic equality; basic needs met; race, gender, and sexual orientation equality; mutuality; no culture of violence; reduce realm of unknown and unpredictable; communication between conflicting parties; transparency in government; well-lit communities; presumption of innocence; accountability; doing away with the callousness of systems; intentional communities; access to ombudsmen-type resources; strong families; challenging the concept of nuclear family and invisible violence; protection from harmful individuals; community conflict resolution; legal control over one's body; fewer weapons; community autonomy; strong infrastructure; intelligent organization of communities for bikes and walkers; access to clean water.

This exercise, and the context in which it occurred, offers a number of insights into local resistance. First, as would become increasingly clear over the years to follow, the nature of space and frame matter. That fall, when the LCCJCB hosted the four meetings in official county political chambers, DLC was forced to speak in confined segments, often responded to questions posed by county officials, and ceded both the opening and closing of the meeting, and thus the meeting's framing, to its organizers. In contrast, the May 3rd event occurred in a radical community space already aligned with community organizing and activism and followed the agenda and framing of its activist organizers. That is, conversations about what kept people safe did not become a rhetorical game of budgets and evidence-based practices. Instead, when officials and civic leaders participated, it was on the rhetorical ground set out by DLC.

Second, the framing of the conversation had implications beyond the actual meeting. As county council president Brian Mulvaney would confirm to me over a year later during our interview, it was that very conversation about safety that he credited with disrupting his own understandings of policing and incarceration. He found himself asking critical questions of whether and how the police bring safety and about whether more cells and more police necessarily equal a safer community. A one-time outspoken supporter for the justice campus, Mulvaney credited DLC's organizing with intervening into the problematic logic by which he had abided and ultimately mitigating his support for the campus.

In a conversation with DLC member Michaela Davis, she attributed Mulvaney's and other's changed perspectives to the ways in which DLC consistently placed the campus in the broader context of mass incarceration. In doing so, Davis argued, the organization made it possible for some officials, who previously had been ardent expansion supporters, to instead break from the narrative of community exceptionalism in which the justice campus was a logical outcome. In her experiences in county meetings, Davis noted to me, "the ways that people justified policy, and the rhetoric that they feel like they have to fit into in order to support a policy, really seems to have this intense Springfield pride and sense of exceptionalism and also doesn't allow for analysis of power or oppression." In centering power and oppression into their intervention, DLC offered a counter-discourse of the campus, which succeeded at times in replacing the discourse of exceptionalism.

Third, this exercise and the conversation it fostered brought DLC and the community into conversation with a transnational network of people fighting similar issues. The idea of reframing issues of safety in order to disrupt the narrative that equated safety with more police and prisons came from activist trainings that some DLC members had participated in with Critical Resistance, the Prison Moratorium Project,[13] and other national groups focused on abolition. Realizing that fighting jail expansion in a Midwestern and liberal community didn't isolate DLC, but rather connected them to communities around the country and beyond, proved to be a motivating and energizing

---

[13]See http://www.calipmp.org/

factor for the group. On the night of May 3rd, after a full day of workshops, a national organizer with the prison abolitionist group Critical Resistance spoke to the remaining attendees. The large pads of paper from the day's discussions still lined the walls of the back room. During the organizer's talk that evening, she glanced around and noted that "I've been to Argentina, Brazil, and everywhere these conversations (about safety) are the same." Later that summer, ten DLC members traveled together to CR10, Critical Resistance's 10-year anniversary conference, to speak on a panel with groups from other communities about respective campaigns against jail expansion.

RESISTING RADICAL RESISTANCE:
THE CASE OF THE "TIRE SLASH TASKFORCE'

Decarcerate Lincoln County resisted the justice campus through direct challenges to constructions of local carceral practices and the processes of decision-making, as well as through counter-hegemonic constructions of certain key concepts on which carcerality was predicated, such as safety. But there were other ways in which people in the community made their opposition to the discourse and the political process known, including an action that occurred while many people were in county chambers for the fourth and final LCCJCB justice campus meeting in the late fall of 2008.

That same evening, perhaps just as PARI representative Richard Kemp was displaying to attendees his maps of the possibilities for carceral expansion, an anonymous group of individuals calling itself the Springfield Tire Slash Taskforce flattened eight tires on multiple vehicles belonging to Lincoln County Community Corrections. The timing of their strike was unmistakable: the group's act of sabotage was meant to display not only local resistance to the justice campus proposal and its contents but also defiance of the premise of the process. While DLC members opted to engage in debate, following the very scripted and proscribed ways in which the county accommodated dissent, other actors celebrated anonymous acts of rebellion at the same time, refusing to acquiesce to a process akin to Mitchell and Staeheli's (2005, 797) "permitted protests":

> The tools [used to construct the contemporary landscape of permitted protest] are used not to silence dissent outright, but rather to regulate it in such a way that dissent can be fully incorporated into, and become part of, the liberal democratic state.

The action by the Tire Slash Taskforce communicated resistance to carcerality as it also rejected the façade of democratic process embodied in the meetings. In a post to an anarchist news website, an anonymous writer relayed the events and the group's analysis:[14]

> In the late hours of Thursday Dec. 11th, the Springfield Tire Slash Taskforce targeted a number of vehicles belonging to Lincoln County Community Corrections. Community Corrections in Lincoln County is responsible for, among many other things, extracting upwards of $200,000 worth of slave labor out of over-policed and over-incarcerated communities of Lincoln County each year.

> This action was taken on the night that the jail building consulting firm PARI presented its master plan to the County and the public for an expanded "justice campus".

> We hope that this action: a) ushered in a fun filled weekend of changing tires for the fascists at Community Corrections and b) sent a message to the county that their plans for expansion and imprisonment won't be tolerated.

In targeting community corrections specifically, the group also resisted the specific carceral imagination of the county that frequently positioned community corrections, and a community corrections ethos, at the center of their plans for expansion. Indeed, even people critical of the overall justice campus plan often stated their enthusiastic support for work release and other community corrections programs. The Tire Slash Taskforce's targeted resistance to "slave labor" extracted by "fascists at Community Corrections", and their warning that expansion would not be tolerated, put forward an insurrectionary and defiant envisioning of the jail and the work release center as equally repressive carceral institutions.

Though infrequent, there have been other displays of more confrontational resistance against incarceration. In June 2008, an unpermitted march broke off from a gathering of activists to protest Interstate 69. Chanting, drumming and carrying torches through the streets of downtown Springfield, the march caught

---

[14]See www.Infoshop.org

the attention of the police. The marchers wound their way through downtown and ended up outside of the county jail. Another anonymous post to the same anarchist website relayed what occurred:[15]

> Anti-I69 activists staged a raucous torch-lit march through the streets of downtown Springfield on Saturday evening to protest the arrest of two tree-sitters and six ground supporters at an I-69 construction site...Torches lit up the night sky at the Saturday action. Activists carried banners, banged drums and set off bottle rockets. Springfield police remained on the sidelines as activists took the streets...As they passed the jail, activists taunted the police with "no more roads, no more jails," "you can't put our friends in jail, we will drive the final nail," and "we will win!"

The demonstration offered a visible connection between seemingly disparate and unaffiliated campaigns and for the ways it challenged the physical boundaries between incarcerated and non-incarcerated spaces. In other words, in these two actions I read important insights into how resistance to local carcerality was, in some ways, a contest to dominant articulations of geographical and cultural boundaries.[16]

CONCLUSIONS: CONTESTING CARCERAL CARTOGRAPHIES

One of the central points to emerge from my time in the field is that the hegemony of mass incarceration inscribed into the community habitus a set of bounded dispositions toward problems of carcerality. As I mentioned in the introduction to this essay, as far back as the late 1970s county officials and residents had been discussing, and practicing, carceral expansion. The institutions that occupied substantial *intellectual* space in the realm of possible solutions to questions of social control and treatment also would take up substantial *physical* space in the actual community. Of course, as long as carceral expansion has been discussed and enacted, community members have resisted.

The discursive and material reality (and their mutually constitutive nature) of the contest over county carcerality resonates

---

[15] Ibid.
[16] A different analysis focused on the geography of protest could also consider the ways in which this action resists the permitted protests analyzed in Mitchell and Staeheli (2005).

with Mitchell's (2000, 5) descriptions of "culture wars" over public spaces:

> Like other wars, wars over culture are territorial; they literally take place...Culture wars are about defining what is legitimate in a society, who is an "insider" and who is an "outsider." They are about determining the social boundaries that govern our lives.

The dominant narrative of the justice campus existed only through the invocation of certain boundaries. Officials imagined a geographical-cultural boundary that distinguished the carceral capabilities of Lincoln County from other localities and the larger state and nation. County council member Reuben Davison specifically identified the prison industrial complex as something *out there*, as geographically outside of the boundaries of the county. Resistance to the campus pointed to it's location as a part of the prison industrial complex, adopting, if reformulating, mass incarceration's logics in its own articulations of carceral expansion.

The two actions I describe above contest dominant boundaries of both space and identity. In the march outside of the jail, community activists breached a boundary between incarcerated and free space; according to at least two respondents, the chanting outside of the jail that night elicited noticeable noise from the inside, most likely prisoners banging on the windows, one of the few ways they could communicate to the outside. This activity across the jail boundary raises important questions about the possibilities of reclaiming carceral space. If DLC's presence in county chambers constituted an intervention into the discourse, but one perhaps ultimately muted by the political-spatial contours of the space, perhaps the action outside of the jail (or, for that matter, the action against community corrections vehicles) suggests other ways (albeit riskier, more confrontational, and perhaps ultimately too decentralized) to construct or occupy counter-hegemonic space.[17]

---

[17] Dylan Rodriguez (2001) provides some insight into understanding these capabilities in his moving account of the convergence of the New York Campaign to Free Angela Davis on the sidewalk outside the women's house of detention where Davis was incarcerated. He writes that the protest disrupted and altered the geography of the prison, an act that has implications for "subversive collective agency in the face of the U.S. gulag" and which demonstrates, through politicizing both the jail and the sidewalk outside of it, "a form of resistance and radicalism that *occupied* a new political space while *constructing* it though physical and oral acts of disruption (Rodriguez, 2001, p. 54). Rodriguez goes on to suggest that the protest implicated the possibilities for convergences and solidarities between prisoners and non-prisoners in

Contests over space and spatial boundaries also can challenge normative definitions around identities.[18] In the actions against Community Corrections vehicles, which were undeniably illegal, activists demonstrated not only resistance to the justice campus proposal and the proceedings but also contested the boundary between criminal and non-criminal. With this action, the Taskforce perhaps articulated identification with the people inside the jail rather than the people inside county chambers who were discussing and debating the justice campus. In the second example of the march, the protesters at the jail had splintered off from an anti-I-69 gathering. In moving between eco-defense and anti-globalization organizing on the one hand to anti-jail resistance on the other, activists challenged the bounded nature of classifications and definitions as they also symbolically demonstrated the interconnectedness of issues.[19]

Finally, Mitchell's usage of "culture wars" as an analytic to examine contests over "social boundaries" offers a specific insight for efforts to destabilize the carceral habitus of Monroe County. One of the ways in which to contest the unquestioned nature of carceral institutions and to intervene in the multiple narratives that posit them as the only response to various questions of space, programs, violence, and safety, is to envision, propose and construct alternative physical landscapes to replace imagined carceral structures.

---

a way that "denaturalizes" the physical space and "deconstructs the institutional integrity/authority of the prison, resulting in a fleeting formation of a strategic trench from which both imprisoned and free can sustain a Gramscian war of position *in concert with one another*" (Ibid, emphasis in the original).

[18] See Mitchell (2000, especially pages 57-76) for a poignant discussion of culture, space, and identity.

[19] Here, New Social Movement (NSM) theory and research illustrates how notions of power and constructions of group process may link groups with seemingly disparate political agendas. Schiffman (1991), in her study of peace activism, found that a group involved in direct action and heavily concerned with process might identify more strongly with a pro-choice movement that has similar "protest politics" than with another peace group focused on lobbying or consciousness-raising. Schiffman (1991, p. 76) articulates this tendency as being about power:

> Movements are defined as much by their assumptions about power as by an issue like peace or feminism. Power is probably the central category for understanding NSMs. It enables us to distinguish NSMs from movements, like labor, that have more traditional understandings of power relations.

This diverse intermingling of the Left also fits within Laclau and Mouffe's (1985) adamancy that radical democracy must replace a universal political economy analysis as the Left's hegemonic articulation.

After the defeat of the justice campus proposal, members of DLC who were involved in other local campaigns around community sustainability participated in discussions with prominent local environmental design activists to imagine an alternative future for the 85-acre site. In the following email to activists, a prominent practitioner of permaculture, an ecological design practice for sustainable living, offered a preliminary analysis of the possibilities at the site:

> The aim is to design the 85 acres to meet many of the community's needs...include[ing] the training and deployment of new urban garden farmers, increasing the number and scale of community garden plots, the creation of food processing and distribution hubs, more space for year around agriculture, space for business incubation, year around farmers market with roofed sales shelters, cold storage and root cellars, orchards, aquaculture, vineyards, mycoculture, seedbanks and arboretum...The design I'm contemplating could add more resilience to our local food economics, train more farmer / growers, help to reskill our local culture and create jobs, manage runoff and catchment of millions of gallons of water high in the landscape (with gravity flow to growers and other users) along with a multitude of additional yields over time.

Thus, inscribed onto the old site was not only the political-economic history of industrialization and outsourcing; not only the varying iterations of liberal carcerality that political leaders envisioned and that may one day rise; but also a resistant imagining of local food security, sustainability education, water conservation, and even regenerative and green job growth.

This article has presented moments of resistance that permeated, disrupted, and occasionally rejected carceral discourses and projects. These moments occurred discursively, such as the challenges activists made to the rhetorics of the justice campus and community decision-making. Moments of resistance also reshaped the meaning of issues on which carcerality had been predicated, forcing carceral projects to lose momentum and legitimacy.

Perhaps most devastating to carceral expansion, resistance can take the form of re-imagining once-carceral space, disrupting incarceration's inevitability and offering a counter-hegemonic cartography. In Audre Lorde's terms, resistance can dismantle the carceral house with new tools. In the case of Lincoln County and the prospect for a permaculture-designed space, local activists re-imagined the bricks and mortar of the justice campus as the rainwater catchment barrels, compost piles, and garden beds of a sustainable community landscape.

REFERENCES

Alexander, M. (2010). *The New Jim Crow: Mass incarceration in the age of colorblindness*. New York, NY: The New Press.

Appadurai, A. (1996). *Modernity at large: Cultural dimensions of globalization.* Minneapolis, MN: University of Minnesota Press.

Austin, J. & Irwin J. (2001). *It's about time: America's imprisonment binge.* Belmont, CA: Wadsworth.

Ball, J., Caldwell, W., & Pranis, K. (2010). *Doing democracy with Circles: Engaging communities in public planning.* St. Paul, MN: Living Justice Press.

Bourdieu, P. (1977). *Outline of a theory of practice.* New York, NY: Cambridge University Press.

Bourdieu, P. (1990) *The logic of practice.* New York, NY: Polity Press.

Bourdieu, P. (1991). *Language and symbolic power.* Cambridge, MA: Harvard University Press.

Bourdieu, P. (2005). Habitus. In J. Hillier & E. Rooksby, (Eds.). *Habitus: A sense of place* (pp.43-52). Burlington, VT: Ashgate.

Clear, T. (2007). *Imprisoning communities: How mass incarceration makes disadvantaged neighborhoods worse.* New York, NY: Oxford University Press.

Clifford, J. & Marcus, G.E. (1986). *Writing culture: The poetics and politics of ethnography.* Berkeley, CA: University of California Press.

Currie, E. (1998). *Crime and punishment in America: Why the solutions to America's most stubborn social crisis have not worked—and what will.* Henry Holt and Company, Inc.

Donziger, S.R., (Ed.) (1996). *The Real war on crime: The report of the National Criminal Justice Commission.* New York, NY: Harper Perennial.

Garland, D. (2001). *The Culture of control: Crime and social order in contemporary society.* Chicago: University of Chicago Press.

Geertz, C. (1973). *The Interpretation of culture.* New York, NY: Basic Books.

Gilmore, R. (2007). *Golden gulag: Prisons, surplus, crisis, and opposition in globalizing California.* Berkeley and Los Angeles: University of California Press.

Goffman, E. (1961). *Asylums: Essays on the social situation of mental patients and other inmates*. New York, NY: Anchor Books.

Graeber, D. (2007). Democracy emerges from the space in between, in Fletcher, R. (Ed.) *Beyond resistance: The future of freedom* (pp.75-109). New York: Nova Science Publishers.

Gupta, A. & Ferguson, J., (Eds.) (1997). *Culture, power, place: Explorations in critical anthropology*. Durham, NC: Duke University Press.

Hallet, M.A. (2006). *Private prisons in America: A critical race perspective*. Urbana and Chicago, IL: University of Illinois Press.

James, J. (Ed.) (2002). *States of confinement: Policing, detention, and prisons*. New York, NY: Palgrave Macmillan.

James, J., (Ed.) (2007). *Warfare in the American homeland: Policing and prison in a penal democracy*, Durham, NC: Duke University Press.

Lorde, A. (1984). *Sister outsider: Essays and speeches by Audre Lorde*. Berkeley, CA: The Crossing Press

Loury, G. (2008). *Race, incarceration, and American values*. Boston, MA: MIT Press.

Marcus, G.E. & Fischer, M.M.J. (1986). *Anthropology as cultural critique: An experimental moment in the human sciences*. Chicago, IL: University of Chicago Press.

Mauer, M., & Chesney-Lind, M. (Eds.). (2002). *Invisible punishment: The collateral consequences of mass imprisonment*. New York, NY: New Press.

Mitchell, D. (2000). *Cultural geography: A critical introduction*. Malden, MA: Blackwell Publishers.

Mitchell, D. & Staeheli, L. A. (2005). Permitting protest: Parsing the fine geography of dissent in America. *International Journal of Urban and Regional Research*, 29(4), 796–813.

Muhammad, K.G. (2010). *The Condemnation of blackness: Race, crime, and the making of modern urban America*. Cambridge, MA: Harvard University Press.

Paley, J. (2004). Accountable democracy: Citizens' impact on public decision making in post-dictatorship Chile. *American Ethnologist*, 31(4), 497-513.

Piché, J. & Walby, K. (2010). Problematizing carceral tours. *British Journal of Criminology*, 50(3), 570-581.

Reiman, J. (2000). The Rich get richer and the poor get prison: Ideology, class, and criminal justice (6th edition). Allyn and Bacon

Rodriguez, D. (2001). "The "Question' of prison praxis: Relations of force, social reproduction, points of departure," in S. Martinot, & J. James, (Eds.) *The Problems of resistance* (pp. 46-68). Amherst, NY: Humanity Books.

Schiffman, J. (1991) "Fight the power': Two groups mobilize for peace. In M. Burawoy, (Ed.). *Ethnography unbound: Power and resistance in the modern metropolis* (pp. 58-79). Berkeley, CA: University of California Press.

Scott, J.C. (1985). *Weapons of the weak: Everyday forms of peasant resistance.* New Haven, CT: Yale University Press.

Scott, J.C. (1990). *Domination and the arts of resistance: Hidden transcripts.* New Haven, CT: Yale University Press.

Shelden, R. (2010). *Our punitive society: Race, class, gender and punishment in America.* Long Grove, IL: Waveland Press.

Sloop, J. (1996). The Cultural prison: Discourse, prisoners, and prisons. Tuscaloosa, AL: University of Alabama Press

Smith, M.P. (2001). *Transnational urbanism: Locating globalization,* Malden, MA: Blackwell.

Thompson, J.B. (1984). *Studies in the theory of ideology.* Berkeley, Los Angeles, CA: University of California Press.

Wacquant L.D. (2002). The Curious eclipse of prison ethnography in the age of mass incarceration. *Ethnography* 3, 371-97

Willis, P. (1977). *Learning to labor: How working class kids get working class jobs.* New York, NY: Columbia University Press

Cooperation versus competition in nature and society: The contribution of Piotr Kropotkin to evolutionary theory

URBANO FRA PALEO,
UNIVERSITY OF SANTIAGO DE COMPOSTELA

Concepts usually have multiple lives, yet in their revival they occur in a changed context, due to the time passed or to their application within a different disciplinary approach. Mutual aid, in its contemporary avenues, seems to be one of them.

In 1902 Piotr Alekseevich Kropotkin published the seminal text *Mutual Aid: A Factor of Evolution*, proposing the principle of mutual support both as a law of nature and a factor of evolution. The volume is, actually, a compilation of an earlier series of articles published in *The Nineteenth Century* from September 1890 to June 1896. The alleged motivation for writing was the publication in the same periodical in 1888 by Darwinist Thomas Henry Huxley of the opus *Struggle for Existence and its Bearing upon Man*. The emphasis placed by Huxley on translating struggle for life as competition to explain one of the three pillars of the theory of evolution—survival of the fittest—pushed Kropotkin to react. He not only was supporting his social theory but was also contributing the results obtained from his exploring expeditions.

The birth and growth of Russian geography as a discipline was closely associated to the expansion of the Russian Empire to the Pacific Ocean throughout Siberia and Central Asia. Peter the Great, in the 18th century, promoted multiple expeditions to survey the country's natural resources (Hooson 1968) and, gradually, dominate increasingly vast territories. Travel, carto-

graphic survey, and narratives served both the scientific interests of the academy and the political interests of the imperialist
tsarist system. Kropotkin, as a military person, served these interests as well.

Kropotkin extensively travelled and explored throughout
Eastern Siberia and Northern Manchuria and learned about the
complex relationships between man and nature, and about the
adaptation of multiple species to those harsh environments. His
early anarchist activism as a writer and the label of revolutionist
have—since the beginning—eclipsed an experienced and long-
lived field work which allowed him to gain a deep understanding of boreal and steppe ecosystems. However, one of the major
theoretical contributions of Kropotkin was in the field of evolutionary theory, suggesting that cooperation within a group explains natural selection of species more satisfactorily than competition—proposed by Darwin but augmented by multiple seminal exegetes—between individuals, although not excluding the
role of the former process. The circumstance that both the articles and the book were published in English by a western publisher—together with the ideological leadership of Kropotkin—
meant that his work was not largely ignored as happened with
many other authors from the Russian school of thought in evolutionary theory (Lapenis 2002).

COOPERATION AS A LAW OF NATURE AND A FACTOR OF EVOLUTION

In his introduction to the revised edition of *Mutual Aid, a
Factor of Evolution* in 1902 Kropotkin enlarged the original title to *Mutual Aid as a Law of Nature and a Factor of Evolution*,
laying emphasis on the basic principle proposed. Kropotkin not
only pairs it to the law of mutual struggle but attributes it much
greater importance:

> ...we may safely say that mutual aid is as much a law of animal life
> as mutual struggle, but that, as a factor of evolution, it most prob-
> ably has a far greater importance...
>
> Sociability is as much a law of nature as mutual struggle...
> (Kropotkin 1902, n.p.)

Indistinctly, sometimes he refers to mutual aid or, at times, to
sociability. He understands that species are determined to live

in society, and suggests that sociability has an innate character and is not an exception:

> Sociability that is, the need of the animal of associating with its like...
>
> ...life in societies is no exception in the animal world; it is the rule, the law of Nature... (Kropotkin 1902, n.p.)

Sociability is neither exclusive to nor has its origin in the human species, nor are social animals building complex societies—such as ants and bees—the only suitable examples, for Kropotkin judges other species' behavior as purposeful and the result of the historical process of evolution:

> The more strange was it to read in the previously-mentioned article by Huxley the following paraphrase of a well-known sentence of Rousseau: "The first men who substituted mutual peace for that of mutual war whatever the motive which impelled them to take that step created society" (*Nineteenth Century*, Feb. 1888, 165). Society has not been created by man; it is anterior to man.
>
> ...it is not imposed, as is the case with ants and bees, by the very physiological structure of the individuals; it is cultivated for the be-nefits of mutual aid... (Kropotkin 1902, n.p.)

Despite his fierce reaction against the arguments of Thomas Henry Huxley in favor of competition, his support of cooperation is not basically naïve, because he also argues against the harmonic view built by Rousseau:

> But it may be remarked at once that Huxley's view of nature had as little claim to be taken as a scientific deduction as the opposite view of Rousseau, who saw in nature but love, peace, and harmony destroyed by the accession of man.
>
> ...neither Rousseau's optimism nor Huxley's pessimism can be accepted as an impartial interpretation of nature. (Kropotkin 1902, n.p.)

Although he believes evolutionists—including Herbert Spencer—might accept his theory, he also believes Spencer would not accept it to be applicable to humankind, for Kropotkin understands that sociability develops increasing complexity and ultimately consciousness. Thus, he considers conflict would be the preferred interpretation of earlier human societies:

> Association is found in the animal world at all degrees of evolution; and, according to the grand idea of Herbert Spencer, so brilliantly developed in Perrier's *Colonies Animales*, colonies are at the very origin of evolution in the animal kingdom. But, in proportion as we ascend the scale of evolution, we see association growing more and more conscious.

> ...there are a number of evolutionists who may not refuse to admit the importance of mutual aid among animals, but who, like Herbert Spencer, will refuse to admit it for Man. For primitive Man they maintain war of each against all was the law of life. (Kropotkin 1902, n.p.)

Piotr Kropotkin became acquainted with the concept of mutual aid in 1883 after Karl Fiodorovich Kessler, who first proposed it in a lecture in January 1880. According to Kropotkin the co-operation-based evolution paradigm was generally accepted in Russian Darwinism:

> Kessler's ideas were so welcomed by the Russian Darwinists, whilst like ideas are not in vogue amidst the followers of Darwin in Western Europe. (Kropotkin 1902, n.p.)

On the contrary, Todes (1989) finds an almost general rejection of the political doctrine formulated by Thomas Robert Malthus in Russian Darwinism, and Kropotkin is not an exception. This is due, according to Todes, to the challenging and difficult assumption of a western-culture concept—struggle for existence —by an eastern culture with a very dissimilar social structure, political history and environmental conditions.

> Because political, linguistic, and cultural barriers existed between Russia and the rest of the world through most of the twentieth century, many of their concepts—with the possible exception of ideas by Kropotkin—are not well known in Western science. On the other hand, some of their ideas are considered to be common knowledge and are not associated with the names of these scientists, who first introduced them. (Lapenis 2002)

Accordingly, cooperation is a concept born in eastern evolutionary thought led by the pair Kessler-Kropotkin. Although it should be noted the key role of German-origin academics in the Russian intelligentsia and in putting up Russian universities at that time.

Kropotkin seemingly agrees with the standard formulated principle of struggle for life because he incorporates the term profusely, but he offers a completely different interpretation of its outcome, questioning its operation through competition and who is the survivor: "Life is struggle; and in that struggle the fittest survive" (Kropotkin 1902, n.p.).

He recognizes competition among plants but not amongst animals, who can move or migrate. Thus, migration acts as a vent to relieve pressure in view of resource scarcity and to avoid clashes:

> However severe the struggle between plants and this is amply proved we cannot but repeat Wallace's remark to the effect that "plants live where they can," while animals have, to a great extent, the power of choice of their abode.

> The importance of migration and of the consequent isolation of groups of animals, for the origin of new varieties and ultimately of new species, which was indicated by Moritz Wagner, was fully rec-ognized by Darwin himself.

> Most of our birds slowly move southwards as the winter comes, or gather in numberless societies and undertake long journeys and thus avoid competition.

> Most of our birds slowly move southwards as the winter comes, or gather in numberless societies and undertake long journeys and thus avoid competition. (Kropotkin 1902, n.p.)

Or, instead, species can adapt to new food sources:

> It is known that portions of a given species will often take to a new sort of food. (Kropotkin 1902, n.p.)

Particularly the new-born, who need to find their niche:

> The new-comers went away before having grown to be competitors. It is evident that if such is the case with men, it is still more the case with animals. (Kropotkin 1902, n.p.)

This view was opposite to that of Darwin, who "maintained a limited but controlling view of ecology as a world stuffed full of competing species—so balanced and so crowded that a new form could only gain entry by literally pushing a former inhabi-tant out" (Gould 1997, n.p.).

Kropotkin deems competition not sufficiently documented by Charles Darwin—or his contemporary Alfred Russel Wal-lace—who did not provide conclusive examples of its opera-tion, for they illustrate the principle with domesticated species:

> But when we look in his work for real proofs of that competition,
> we must confess that we do not find them sufficiently convincing.

> ...its value is impaired by its being taken from among domesticated
> animals. (Kropotkin 1902, n.p.)

In his argumentation he is very careful to avoid departure
from mainstream Darwinism and argues that the term struggle
for life is used both by Darwin and Wallace in a metaphorical
sense, aligned with his acceptance of the principle of struggle
for life:

> The term "struggle for life" is again used in its metaphorical sense,
> and may have no other.

> ..."struggle for existence," evidently applies to the word "extermin-
> ation" as well. It -can by no means be understood in its direct sense,
> but must be taken "in its metaphoric sense."

> As to "competition," this expression, too, is continually used by
> Darwin (see, for instance, the paragraph "On Extinction") as an im-
> age, or as a way-of-speaking, rather than with the intention of con-
> veying the idea of a real competition between two portions of the
> same species for the means of existence. (Kropotkin 1902, n.p.)

It was not until Darwin wrote *The Descent of Man, and Selection in Relation to Sex* in 1871 that he provided examples of
various other species and finally elaborated his own view of the
concept of struggle for live. Glassman (2000) believes that Darwin's focus on competition allowed him to neglect the existence of cooperation. According to Kropotkin, Darwin considers competition to be intraspecific:

> The idea which permeates Darwin's work is certainly one of real
> competition going on within each animal group for food, safety,
> and possibility of leaving an offspring. (Kropotkin 1902, n.p.)

But the examples provided are—yet again for Kropotkin—not
sufficiently illustrative to derive a general law:

> The struggle between individuals of the same species is not illus-
> trated under that heading by even one single instance: it is taken as
> granted; and the competition between closely-allied animal species
> is illustrated by but five examples, out of which one, at least (relat-
> ing to the two species of thrushes), now proves to be doubtful.
> (Kropotkin 1902, n.p.)

And although Kropotkin accepts a low-intensity competition
for resources limited in time: "there is, within each species, a

certain amount of real competition for food at least, at certain periods" (Kropotkin 1902, n.p.). He alleges not having found any examples of intraspecific competition: "I failed to find struggle for the means of existence, among animals belonging to the same species" (Kropotkin 1902, n.p.).

Instead, Kropotkin relies on group selection, according to the dominant explanatory paradigm in the first half of the 20th century (van Schaik and Kappeler 2006). Although Kropotkin greatly emphasizes the role of cooperation he does not completely exclude competition nor does he oppose natural selection, and understands that both operate simultaneously, "competition is not the rule either in the animal world or in mankind" (Kropotkin 1902, n.p.).

According to Gould (1997) this was the main contribution made by this thinker to the evolutionary theory. Kropotkin did not radically opposed Darwinism but widened its scope, identifying the significance of a complementary but lessened mechanism. And, if he overemphasized cooperation, "most Darwinians in Western Europe had exaggerated competition just as strongly" (Gould 1997), and "therefore created a dichotomy within the general notion of struggle – two forms with opposite import: (1) organism against organism of the same species for limited resources, leading to competition; and (2) organism against environment, leading to cooperation" (Gould 1997, n.p.). Kropotkin understands that struggle takes place between the group and a changing environment that threatens survival:

> One species succumbs, not because it is exterminated or starved out by the other species, but because it does not well accommodate itself to new conditions, which the other does. (Kropotkin 1902, n.p.)

He contends competition does not satisfactorily explain which individuals survive, while the principle of cooperation satisfactorily explains the survival of a variety of groups, since species may benefit more from their sociability than from their physical aptitudes:

> ...the fittest are not the physically strongest, nor the cunningest, but those who learn to combine so as mutually to support each other, strong and weak alike, for the welfare of the community.

> The fittest are thus the most sociable animals, and sociability appears as the chief factor of evolution, both directly, by securing the

well-being of the species while diminishing the waste of energy, and indirectly, by favouring the growth of intelligence.

> Those species which willingly or unwillingly abandon it are doomed to decay; while those animals which know best how to combine, have the greatest chances of survival and of further evolution, although they may be inferior to others in each of the faculties enumerated by Darwin and Wallace, save the intellectual faculty.

> ...we maintain that under any circumstances sociability is the greatest advantage in the struggle for life. (Kropotkin 1902, n.p.)

Kropotkin opposes the principle of the survival of the fittest, a term coined by Herbert Spencer but not adopted by Darwin until the fifth edition of his work *The Origin of Species* in 1869, after having been convinced by Alfred Russel Wallace (Leonard 2009):

> Those who survive a famine, or a severe epidemic of cholera, or small-pox, or diphtheria, such as we see them in uncivilized countries, are neither the strongest, nor the healthiest, nor the most intelligent.

In some way his argumentation seems to be inspired by religious or moral values, advancing some of the ethical principles later compiled in his work *Ethics: Origin and Development*, published posthumously in 1924:

> The higher conception of "no revenge for wrongs," and of freely giving more than one expects to receive from his neighbours, is proclaimed as being the real principle of morality

> ...even the new religions have only reaffirmed that same principle. They found their first supporters among the humble, in the lowest, downtrodden layers of society, where the mutual-aid principle is the necessary foundation of every-day life... (Kropotkin 1924, n.p.)

Thus, Kropotkin explicitly manifested his agreement with the theory of evolution proposed by Charles Darwin, regardless of his critical perspective of competition as a motor of change, but belligerently wrote against his epigones:

> It happened with Darwin's theory as it always happens with theories having any bearing upon human relations. Instead of widening it according to his own hints, his followers narrowed it still more. (Kropotkin 1902, n.p.)

He firmly opposed both Malthus and Huxley—but particularly the first, despite the trigger of the series of papers being

Huxley's writing—because he believed the notion of competition grew from Malthusianism. In the same vein, he contended Malthus led Darwin to a powerful, and ultimately erroneous, view of the factors of evolution, "originated from the narrow Malthusian conception of competition between each and all" (Kropotkin 1902, n.p.).

His basic argumentation against Malthusianism is grounded in the role of the environment, and the climatic conditions above all, as a principal limiting factor, while diminishing the influence of the scarcity of resources.

THE ENVIRONMENT AS A FACTOR OF EVOLUTION

Kropotkin is optimistic for he observes that in extensive geographical areas competition is not observed, since there are sufficient resources available:

> The actual numbers of animals in a given region are determined, not by the highest feeding capacity of the region, but by what it is every year under the most unfavourable conditions. So that, for that reason alone, competition hardly can be a normal condition; but other causes intervene as well to cut down the animal population below even that low standard.

> ...we can safely say that their numbers are not kept down by competition; that at no time of the year they can struggle for food, and that if they never reach anything approaching to over-population, the cause is in the climate, not in competition...

> "Don't compete! competition is always injurious to the species, and you have plenty of resources to avoid it." (Kropotkin 1902, n.p.)

However he did not develop his idea much further, as Todes (1989) observes. Kropotkin understands the important role of the environment as a driver of species evolution, only tempered by cooperation among individuals, and he illustrates it with examples from human society and social animals:

> We understood them as continued endeavours as a struggle against adverse circumstances for such a development of individuals, races, species and societies...

> Sociability thus puts a limit to physical struggle, and leaves room for the development of better moral feelings. (Kropotkin 1902, n.p.)

Hence, he understands struggle for life as *struggle against nature*, with species confronting variability and extreme changes in the form of natural hazards:

> ...physical changes are continually going on in every given area...
>
> For industrial progress, as for each other conquest over nature, mutual aid and close intercourse certainly are, as they have been, much more advantageous than mutual struggle. (Kropotkin 1902, n.p.)

Disasters periodically cause loss of lives, controlling population sizes, a factor not sufficiently taken into account by Malthus, and therefore diminishing the validity of his principle of overpopulation:

> ...against an inclement Nature enormous destruction of life which periodically results from natural agencies...
>
> The importance of natural checks to over-multiplication, and especially their bearing upon the competition hypothesis, seems never to have been taken into due account. (Kropotkin 1902, n.p.)

The dimension of environmental changes exceeds in most cases human capacity to dominate nature, showing that this cannot be tamed:

> However, it is unfortunately characteristic of human nature gladly to believe any affirmation concerning men being able to change at will the action of the forces of Nature (Kropotkin 1902, n.p.)

But, conversely, environmental change also turns into an opportunity, because it weakens competitors:

> Each storm, each inundation, each visit of a rat to a bird's nest, each sudden change of temperature, take away those competitors which appear so terrible in theory. (Kropotkin 1902, n.p.)

And this is how environmental variability does not have an exclusive role in evolution because, if this were the case, instead of progression there would be regression:

> But if the evolution of the animal world were based exclusively, or even chiefly, upon the survival of the fittest during periods of calamities; if natural selection were limited in its action to periods of exceptional drought, or sudden changes of temperature, or inundations, retrogression would be the rule in the animal world. (Kropotkin 1902, n.p.)

His approach is aligned with that prevailing in the Russian school of Geography—Kropotkin was himself not only a naturalist or a geographical explorer but a geographer, in the scientific context of the 19th century—concerned about the transformations of natural landscapes and about the impact of man on nature (Hooson 1968). Todes (1989) argues that Kropotkin saw himself as a successor of a tradition that ranged across various ideological stances. The large and sparsely populated land of Siberia was being explored, mapped and settled, steered by a sustained Russian policy since the 18th century, and those untouched natural landscapes would become eventually dramatically transformed. In this scholarly tradition, climate is considered to be the primary factor, according to Kropotkin, "the cause is in the climate, not in competition" (Kropotkin 1902, n.p.).

Almost all Russian Darwinists agree on a radical refutation of the Malthusian standpoint on the role of overpopulation in evolution through competition (Todes 1989), understanding that overpopulation had not a *raison d'être* in an outsized Russian back country (Gould 1991), and recognizing that "Malthus makes a far better prophet in a crowded, industrial country professing an ideal of open competition in free markets" (Gould 1991, 333). In this vein *Mutual Aid, a factor of evolution* came to synthesize mainstream Russian criticism (Gould 1991).

KROPOTKIN AND SOCIAL DARWINISM

Some may argue Kropotkin's reaction was against social Darwinism, but Leonard (2009) contends that he could not oppose it because social Darwinism had almost no currency before 1916. The paradox, according to Leonard, is that when Richard Hofstadter declared social Darwinism an extinct social philosophy, the term began to gain an unexpected vigor that it did not have during its pretended dawn and maturity. Hence, although both Kropotkin and Hofstadter opposed social Darwinism, the first did not deny the translation of Darwinism to social ideology, while the second firmly opposed its applicability to social issues. Although both fought the principles of social Darwinism and competitive individualism, they do not agree upon the relationships among natural and social sciences. Hofstadter thought that "Man's task is not to imitate the laws of nature but to observe them, appropriate them, direct them" (Hofstadter 1944, 58). Hofstadter was a determined fighter against the translation of biology to human life through his work *Social Darwinism in American Thought, 1860–1915*, published in 1944, but in his task he ended with an unreasonable position. "what Hofstadter condemned as biological determinism, he proposed to substitute the opposite extreme, cultural determinism, the idea that biology has nothing to do with human action" (Leonard 2009, 39).

Kropotkin wrote *Mutual Aid* to oppose an emerging discourse and helped to cut the grass below the feet of an evolving doctrine, while Hofstadter reanimated the concept, although not the ideology. Neither Herbert Spencer nor William Graham Sumner used the term social Darwinism in all their writings —they even rarely cite Darwin—(Leonard 2009), and this is how Ruse (1980) deems Hofstadter meant social Spencerism instead of social Darwinism. Leonard (2009, 40) believes Herbert Spencer would himself have rejected the label Darwinist, "in part because his own theory of evolution differed from and was published before Darwin's" in 1852.

Leonard (2009, 47) maintains that some scholars consider: "Not only is the Darwin of the *Descent of Man* a social Darwinist, but so too is the Darwin of *The Origin of Species*, which contains no references to homo sapiens." Nevertheless this is not the case for Kropotkin. But they might agree that "it was classical political economy that influenced the theorists of organic evolution rather than the other way around" (Leonard, 2009, 48).

According to Hawley (1999) cooperation can be understood as a form of competition. She contends that—in the end—cooperation works in two ways: "individuals can work together to gain resources otherwise unattainable … or individuals can coordinate their efforts to gain access to resources which in the end are distributed inequitably" (Hawley 1999, 106). This cooperation-as-competition approach argues that a surficial cooperative and prosocial structure is a layer placed on top of the layer of selfish goals (Hawley 1999). And these without doubt emerge. Hawley judges: "Social dominance inevitably results when individuals are unequal in their ability or motivation to acquire and control resources" (Hawley 1999, 122).

Kropotkin adopts a teleological stance when he sees progress, through cooperation, in evolution, for he understands unsocial species do not survive. Unexpectedly he could become Spencerian, and ultimately Lamarckian, opposing one of the three basic principles of Darwinism, random variation:

...the dominating influence of the mutual-aid factor as an element of progress.

The mutual protection which is obtained in this case, the possibility of attaining old age and of accumulating experience, the higher intellectual development, and the further growth of sociable habits, secure the maintenance of the species, its extension, and its further progressive evolution. The unsociable species, on the contrary, are doomed to decay.

...for the success of the struggle for life, and especially for the pro-gressive evolution of the species, is far more important than the law of mutual contest. (Kropotkin 1902, n.p.)

In modern times, the conception of cooperation does not seem to emphasize the influence on species success, as Kropotkin invoked, but its behavioral nature. It comprises both the social interaction and the outcome in terms of benefits and eventual costs (van Schaik and Kappeler 2006). Cooperation is not constrained to intraspecific processes but it is also interspecific (van Schaik and Kappeler 2006), improving the opportunities for the survival of the interacting species. Van Schaik and Kappeler (2006, 5) prefer a broader and more practical definition which excludes altruism, because it would be difficult to estimate whether an act is costly for the actor, and because "it is particularly difficult to explain the existence of behaviors that benefit others at the expense of the ego". Van Schaik and Kappeler (2006) think the examples provided by Kropotkin correspond in broad terms to mutualism, a kind of cooperation in which acts are beneficial for both actor and recipient, and particularly to by-product mutualism.

Kropotkin did not take into consideration other dimensions involved, such as the changes of strategy adopted by individuals over their life span (Hawley 1999), such as the varying levels of cooperativism. But, above all, Kropotkin did not recognize the various threats to cooperation, particularly the various forms of exploitation, in terms of "the vulnerability of the coop-erator to being exploited by selfish partners" (van Schaik and Kappeler 2006, 4). Free riders, lack of timely reciprocity, and risk-avoidance in mutualism expose some social individuals to high risk and are key limiting factors for the extension of cooperation. Its translation to human society not only increases the complexity of the search for explanation but also the adoption of this principle as a basis for governance. The entire work of Kropotkin has a strong ethical focus driven by his political commitment with anarchism, which culminated in the text *Ethics: Origin and Development* (1924), and he judged cooperation was the basis for his ethics:

> In the practice of mutual aid, which we can retrace to the earliest beginnings of evolution, we thus find the positive and undoubted origin of our ethical conceptions; and we can affirm that in the ethical progress of man, mutual support not mutual struggle has had the leading part.

> That mutual aid is the real foundation of our ethical conceptions seems evident enough.

> In the practice of mutual aid, which we can retrace to the earliest beginnings of evolution, we thus find the positive and undoubted origin of our ethical conceptions; and we can affirm that in the ethical progress of man, mutual support—not mutual struggle—has had the leading part.

Despite his origins as a naturalist, Kropotkin rapidly turned into a social thinker who identified cooperation as a basis for social change. And this led him to be an evolutionist more than a revolutionist, despite the title of his memories (*Memories of a Revolutionist*, 1899), for he does not see sudden change in nature a factor of development. While he regrets Darwin did not propose—nor elaborate—the concept of cooperation, Kropotkin himself did not sufficiently elaborate the notion and laid major emphasis on criticizing the pretended predominance of competition. Notwithstanding Kropotkin's major contribution consists in the resolute association of the concept of mutual aid—or, in contemporary terms, cooperation—to evolutionary theory, and its application to the explanation of social processes, and to the elaboration of new forms of political action, particularly through public participation.

REFERENCES

Chappell, J.E. Jr. and I.M. Matley, 1967. "Marxism and Environmentalism." *Annals of the Association of American Geographers*, 57(1): 203-207.

Glassman, M. 2000. "Mutual Aid Theory and Human Development: Sociability as Primary." *Journal for the Theory of Social Behaviour* 30: 4.

Gould, S.J. 1997. "Kropotkin was No Crackpot." *Natural History* 106. http://www.marxists.org/subject/essays/kropotkin.htm

————.1991. *Bully for Brontosaurus: Reflections in Natural History.* London: Penguin. pp. 325-339.

Hawley, P.H. 1999. "The Ontogenesis of Social Dominance: A Strategy-Based Evolutionary Perspective." *Developmental Review* 19: 97–132.

Hofstadter, R. 1944. *Social Darwinism in American Thought, 1860-1915.* Philadelphia: University of Pennsylvania Press.

Hooson, D.J.M. 1968. "The Development of Geography in Pre-Soviet Russia." *Annals of the Association of American Geographers* 58(2): 250-264.

Kappeler, P.M. and C.P. van Schaik (eds), 2006. *Cooperation in Primates and Humans, Mechanisms and Evolution.* Berlin: Springer.

Kropotkin, P. 1902. *Mutual Aid: A Factor of Evolution.* Revised ed. London: William Heinemann. http://socserv.mcmaster.ca/econ/ugcm/3ll3/kropotkin/mutaid.txt

Kropotkin, P. 1924. *Ethics: Origin and Development.* London: Harrap.

Lapenis, A.G. 2002. "Directed Evolution of the Biosphere: Biogeochemical Selection or Gaia?" *The Professional Geographer*, 54(3): 379-391.

Leonard, T.C. 2009. "Origins of the Myth of Social Darwinism: The Ambiguous Legacy of Richard Hofstadter's Social Darwinism in American Thought." *Journal of Economic Behavior & Organization* 71:37-51.

Ruse, M. 1980. "Social Darwinism: Two Sources." *Albion* 12: 23–36.

van Schaik, C.P. and P.M. Kappeler, 2006. "Cooperation in Primates and Humans: Closing the Gap." In *Cooperation in Primates and Humans, Mechanisms and Evolution.* Berlin: Springer. pp. 3-21.

Todes, D.P. 1989. *Darwin without Malthus: The Struggle for Existence in Russian Evolutionary Thought.* Oxford: Oxford University Press.

de Waal, F.B.M. and S.F. Brosnan. 2006. "Simple and Complex reciprocity in primates." In *Cooperation in Primates and Humans, Mechanisms and Evolution.* eds. C.P. van Schaik and P.M. Kappeler. Berlin: Springer. pp. 85-105.

de Waal F.B.M. and Davis, J.M. 2003. "Capuchin cognitive ecology: cooperation based on projected returns." *Neuropsychologia* 41:221-228.

PUNCHING OUT
PRESS.ORG

"Without a strategy that stems from common political agreement, revolutionary organizations are bound to be an affair of reactivism against the continual manifestations of oppression and injustice and/or a cycle of fruitless actions to be repeated over and over again, with little analysis or understanding of the consequences."

- Furious Five Collective,
on Especifismo

free · open
design, distro & incubation
originals & reprints:

*essays · opinion · history · herstory · art ·
tactical manuals · strategic analysis*

**on the web:
PunchingOutPress.org
on twitter:
@punchingout**

[arts]

We are coming... strong... unstoppable: A Global Balkans Interview with Belgrade Artist Milica Ružicić

INTERVIEW BY TAMARA VUKOV, GLOBAL BALKANS,
WITH THE PARTICIPATION OF IVAN ZLATIĆ, POKRET ZA SLOBODU,
AND SAŠA PERIĆ, FILMMAKER
TRANSLATION BY IRINA CERIĆ AND KOLE KILIBARDA, GLOBAL BALKANS
TRANSCRIPTION BY ACO POPADIĆ, KONTRAPUNKT

This interview with Belgrade artist Milica Ružicić focuses on her series of paintings on police brutality in both Serbia and globally that appear in this issue of the Journal of Radical Criminology[1], and which was also the centerpiece of her solo exhibition in the Belgrade Cultural Center (Kulturni Centar Beograd) in November 2010. It was conducted in Belgrade in January 2011 by Tamara Vukov for her feature-length documentary Tranzicija / Transition. Currently in post-production, the film traces the impact of the post-socialist transition to capitalism in Serbia over the course of 5 years from the perspective of those confronting the forces of neoliberal accumulation by dispossession (to cite David Harvey), particularly

---

[1] See the black-and-white reproductions of these paintings on pages 99-115 or go to our website <http://journal.radicalcriminology.org> to see them in full (bloody, intense, living) color.

workers undergoing forced mass privatization and displaced people in the region.
Tamara: Can you talk a bit about what do you do, your art practice?
Milica: I studied sculpture, but this is my first exhibition of paintings. That is perhaps something unusual for sculptors, for sculptors to paint, but for me it isn't because I usually choose which medium to work with intuitively depending on the concept or idea I have. I choose the medium that will best illustrate that particular idea. This means that in addition to sculpture, I've also done performance, video works, photo-montages, so it was totally logical for me to choose to paint at this point as well.
Tamara: So you take a multidisciplinary approach?
Well yes, I approach the work, I don't have one medium in which I constantly work. Depending on my conception, it depends in which medium the work will be best interpreted or read as I have imagined it. From that perspective, I understand the medium not only as a visual language but also as a weapon and tool for reading works.
Tamara: So what brought you to work with painting for this series?
Milica: Well exactly that, I started from the point that I want to paint. This time I inverted my strategy and began with the medium itself. I decided to paint because painting on canvas is a recognizable and the most traditional of artistic media. Today paintings are also popular market commodities that are used as status symbols. Then I started to think about what I wanted the theme of these paintings to be. What was it that I wanted people to look at in this context? I wanted to start from that position, to think about the image as an object for sale and to use it for my own ends, instead of running away from this aspect of its character. For a long time I though about what I wanted someone to hang on their wall and look at, and then, through a bit of research, I came upon the issue of police brutality, which I came to understand as a globally relevant topic. I was particularly interested in the universality of this problem, how it has somehow become the image of global politics today. This image isn't hidden, we see these images in the media, but they are so frequently seen and alternated that their force becomes spent and we

quickly forget about them. I decided that I would take these images from newspapers, the Internet, as evidence of police brutality and transform those images into paintings on canvas, since paintings are objects that imply permanence.

So I made a series of 16 small paintings that are 30 x 40 cm. I deliberately chose a format that could be easily commercialized, since small formats are cheaper and easier to sell. (Belgrade art critic) Jasmina Čubrilo calls these "civic formats" since they are often found on the walls of citizens' apartments. In spite of my efforts to turn these into commercial formats these images weren't easy to look at. They're not something that someone would want to keep on the walls of their house or in their office, since these brutal scenes are unpleasant. Nevertheless, in this way they wouldn't be forgotten. I treated these images like a document, some type of evidence, so in that sense I didn't want to alter them or aestheticize the violence. My only intervention was to remove the background, leaving only a white canvas behind the figures in conflict. I wanted to unify them in this way. These are 16 images from different cities around the world, usually choosing protests where political will or reactions to the political decisions of governments are being suppressed with police violence. That is the first segment of the exhibition.

Then I wanted to add a local story, since this is important for the local public. For this I chose a different format, the museum format of the large historical painting, which in this case was close to 3 x 2 m. The image I chose was the strike of the workers / small shareholders of the Jugoremedija pharmaceutical company, who persistently and resolutely fought to save their factory in an era of bad privatizations, which continue to this day. I chose one scene from Ivan Zlatić's documentary film "Ugovor *na štetu trećeg*" (*Contract Damaging to Third Parties*) that follows this four-year struggle. The chosen scene deals with the forceful intervention of the police at the moment when judicial proceedings were still in progress to determine who actually owns the firm. At this moment, the police intervened, taking the side of the provenly corrupt director and his aggressive private security army (the so-called people in black), in order to evict the workers from the factory. This intervention came in spite of the fact that the workers were the owners of a greater number of shares (58%) of shares than the aforementioned director (42%) and the fact that the workers acted far more responsibly towards their factory than the director did.

In this sense, it became clear that it was necessary to re-examine for whom the police was working, whose interests it was defending. Whether they are defending the rights and freedoms of citizens or the personal interests of powerful individuals? And that's the question that I wanted to become the main thread woven throughout this exhibition, from the small paintings of police brutality in the world to this local story.

That is, therefore, the second part of the exhibition. This large painting is framed in a large golden baroque frame modeled after museum pieces depicting historical events. Why? Because I wanted to take this small segment of modern worker struggles and in some way historicize it, i.e. to write it into historical events, so that it is recorded, remembered and retold. That was my intention, now we will see whether or not it will happen. I remain hopeful.

In the third segment of the exhibition, alongside the large painting depicting Jugoremedija, I displayed Jugoremedija's products. After a long struggle they succeeded in introducing self-management and saving their factory from bankruptcy, even managing to adopt European standards (that were being imposed by the European Union). Not only did I want to display the pharmaceuticals they produce, but I tendentiously chose drugs that serve as painkillers, used to treat pain and injury. It's a cynical answer to all these police beatings, a little ironic twist on the whole issue so that someone can leave the exhibition with a smile.

The fourth segment of the exhibition is the very fabric on which all these pictures were painted. These canvases were produced in a correctional home in Sombor, which means they were made by prisoners. This is why I turned one of the canvases backwards to reveal the stamp showing the origins of this canvas.

Tamara: You've mentioned several times this large painting depicting the local situation and then these other paintings, from other events elsewhere around the globe. Let me ask you then how you see the relationship between the local and the global in this case?

Milica: I think that in the global sense these local policies seem like some type of farce. In principle the conditions are quite similar, though of course the standards differ. People are better off in some places and poorer in others, though even in rich states you'll find many poor people. This means that these differences are often an illusion or to speak as a painter, they are gradations in chiaroscuro or shadings of light and dark. These local stories are in principle very similar, a small number of extremely rich people and a large number of poor people. That's why I wanted to connect them in an exhibition because we can no longer look at politics simply from our own corner, without analyzing what is happening in the rest of the world.

Tamara: Can you talk a little more about your own engagement, particularly in relation to the situation in Jugoremedija?

Milica: Well I wouldn't say I was seriously engaged there. I participated at that time in a video collective, so I happened to be there at the beginning of the Jugoremedija workers' strike. At that time I wasn't very disciplined, it was more impulsive, so I documented the beginnings of that struggle but I didn't end up doing anything with the footage. In fact, they began their strike in 2003, while we as representatives of Drugacije Svet Je Moguce (DSM / Another World Is Possible) as part of the PGA (Peoples' Global Action) meeting organized in Belgrade in 2004 paid them a visit to offer our support. That is when I was introduced to their protest and problems. At the time the situation in the entire country was tragic, all over the place these privatizations and the transition, which led to mass layoffs of workers and the closure of factories and no one knew what would happen to them. We could only hope that they would persist.

Tamara: It's interesting that you're taking about how in the video collective, everything was a bit impulsive, done quickly, and that you eventually came to this more deliberate way of working...

Milica: It is, I was a lot younger then so I wasn't as disciplined. I think I'm more mature now, I hope, and I have more responsibilities, so I've learned to manage my time. Perhaps also because my interest in social issues has become linked to my art practice, so that these are no longer two separate areas of interest.

Tamara: Also, your choice of painting as a medium, it seems to me to constitute a strategy of recontextualization, recontextualizing these images from the media that one sees continuously in a decontextualized way...

Milica: It is, we're saturated with these images and the problem is that this saturation pushes us not to see them anymore. Something happens and it's in the spotlight for maybe a week. In two weeks it's totally forgotten. I think that this media saturation is deliberate, because this is actually easier to ignore... You give everyone the freedom to say anything and then you create so much noise that it's difficult to separate what's important from what's unimportant.

Tamara: One more thing, the exhibition catalogue and the text by Jasmina Čubrilo... at one point she says how this exhibition and your approach fits with the documentary style in an eccentric way. What do you think is eccentric here in your approach to documentary?

Milica: Well, I think that she meant to say that there exists this documentary style in art and that usually it expresses itself through the medium of video or photos, and that we rarely or at least for a long time haven't have seen it in the medium of paintings. Perhaps this combination is a little strange, with pop art, but maybe its not. Now what is eccentric, that varies, maybe in five years from now such an approach will again be quite common.

Tamara: How do you look upon the tradition of socialist realism since it also existed in this region?

Milica: At first when I was looking for models in undertaking a large painterly composition I returned to Rembrandt, who had been dear to me since childhood. I mostly took from him the experience of building a dynamic within the painting - light, movement, drama in general. However, Rembrandt painted during the baroque era, so for his style flamboyance is also important, things like hats and clothing in general. My theme is contemporary, so the clothes of the workers and the police are much closer to socialist realist scenes. Nevertheless, the difference lies in the fact that socialist realism was an artistic tendency that was dictated by the state and was concerned with an idealized representation of communist society and struggle. Since in my painting the police, as a representation of state power, aren't necessarily portrayed in a positive light, perhaps it is best to compare it to Russian critical realism, as represented by Repin, from whom socialist realism originates. Of course I'm totally okay with the idea that everyone can say what they associate it with, because I do not want to impose a single reading upon the audience.

Tamara: I was just thinking about what it is you can take from this series of paintings regarding the role of state violence in this specific historical moment, relative to other times...

Milica: Well, I wouldn't like to impose a conclusion although it can probably be felt... I declare myself to be an anarchist, so for me the state is something not necessarily positive, that is why I like to criticize it. I don't think I know the solution that would bring good for all, which is why I think that everyone must be sufficiently responsible for and interested in deciding upon their fate, instead of some police force, state, or some other structure...The police is a state apparatus, while who exactly controls this apparatus is a subject for reflection.

Tamara: Because as you said, before would there have been such a conflict between the police and workers in the same way?

Milica: I don't know, maybe there were such conflicts, I was born at the end of that time so I can't say exactly. When I listen to stories about that time, they are all subjective angles, sometimes matching up, sometimes conflicting, so I'm not sure what is correct there. Was that really the time of the beautiful life, or did there also then exist reasons for critique? I think that as long as a state exists, there exist reasons to critique it, since its structures are subject to abuse.

Ivan: You said you were an anarchist. Okay. That in your paintings there is an assumption that the state is on the wrong side. That is something that does not need to be overly explained. But still, now that you've commented about this event in Jugoremedija, you cannot avoid the fact that the company director Jovica Stefanović was in the end arrested and brought to justice. Do you sometimes... because I'm looking at these images and wondering why the police is always on the wrong side... do you believe that they will always be on the wrong side, on the side of the stronger party? Or can something be done maybe to change the situation; can it all be turned in some

new direction and are you participating in some type of democratization in that direction, by warning about it?
Milica: That is what critique is for, to fix some mistakes. Of
course, I tendentiously chose those positions where the police is
on the wrong side, since I think that simply this is what I wanted to bring forward as a clear problem in the organization of
this system. So long as there are armed people who have a mo-
nopoly on violence and who represent the state, the abuse of
this position of power will occur. It probably goes without saying that not all police officers will be bad, but there will certainly be those who will do bad things in that position, since they're
in a position that essentially allows them to do that.
Tamara: If we're talking about Jasmina Čubrilo's text, she describes that moment of socialism's reorganization into a capitalist system, of this so-called transition, and that state power
plays a specific role in this transition ...
Milica: ... for this local context. It's sort of a strange situation
became the systemic changes were so sudden, from a system of
relative social security we moved to a system something like,
dare I say it, the "wild west'. Capitalism is understood to require stark class differences, whereas the experience of self-
managing socialism taught that sudden wealth, especially during the wars of the nineties, could not be gotten honestly, that
some plunder or fraud had to be involved. In fact, such people
(the new rich) now function here without much interference,
apparently based on the fact that such behavior is normal under
capitalism. So my take on transition, at least here, is that when
viewed from a critical position founded on notions of social justice and ethics, transition enacts the opposite: uncritical acceptance of the capitalist system and a Machiavellian ethic. Those
generations who lived in and remember a different time are apparently supposed to either die off or to somehow acclimatize
themselves, transforming into people who believe that the criminals, mafiosos and robbers of previous eras have suddenly become successful businessmen, resourceful individuals who can
serve as role models for today's children on the understanding
that the ends justify the means.
Tamara: You've already mentioned that you're not quite from
that generation, but given the prominence of those themes [a

supposed or so-called yugo-nostalgia], can you comment, from your perspective, on that time, on what happened in the SFRJ?
Milica: Well, I'm not even certain exactly how it was, I know it more through the recollections of my parents. They told me about how we would all go to the seaside every year, how there was never a lot but always enough to live on. We never thought about whether my sister and I could both go to university; we had free education so that was a given. My parents didn't live in fear of losing their jobs. We all had health insurance, always. Our passports allowed us to travel anywhere without problems. It seems to me that time and that country were a better place for a young person than where we are now. If I could have chosen to be born in those times, perhaps I would have; that's my thinking, whether or not I'm actually right. As for the break-up of Yugoslavia, I don't think we can analyze local politics outside of global influences, because global events dictate local politics. And in that regard, given the fall of the Berlin Wall and the Iron Curtain, we had had a particular role in that divide as a buffer zone and so we also needed to fall, both because that zone was no longer necessary and because it was a successful example of an alternative which could threaten western capitalism. We also represented a potential new market for the West which could be entered into at very favorable terms, wartime sanctions and the embargo having served their purposes. And then after a few years, the long-awaited foreign investors appeared at the door, gaining access to a new market, real estate and a low-cost workforce, likewise de-valued by years of war.
Ivan: Aside from my disagreement with a version of the dissolution of Yugoslavia in which only external factors exist, I think that there is much that was local, and especially during wartime, local politics persisted. How else can you explain the existence of several hundred prison camps in Bosnia and Herzegovina? That is like a social cancer. That's not something easily explainable, when every village had a prison camp.
Milica: As a matter of principle I see no justification for any of that, I see no justification for war at all, any war. I'm speaking about that which goes along with war, for when war begins it gathers momentum and is very difficult to stop. It becomes revenge for revenge, a cycle of revenge... For me, those responsible are those who start wars, who create the conditions for the

initiation of war, who divide and fan the flames. Once a war begins, nationalism cannot be easily extinguished and it will just
boil up, given the need to take sides, to determine who is with
us and who is against us, to ensure that you do not stand alone,
because then you are a target for everyone. I think that war is
something else, it's the outcome of the underlying fuel, which
only needs a lit match to ignite the madness.

Tamara: To return to your large painting. To me, it seems that
what you are representing is another means and type of war.

Milica: Well yes, it is true. Pretty much every day we are engaged in some type of civil war, or more precisely, a class war,
in which the state constantly visits repression upon its citizens.

Tamara: All the work you've done to produce this painting,
those three or four months. As a symbol, why is it important to
you at this moment?

Milica: The story of Jugoremedija is especially important to
because it had a positive outcome. At least for now. Their story
is symbolic, a story of a revolution that must be continued.
Their example demonstrates how despite lacking overt political
theory and ideology, they found a way to come to collective solutions and to self-organize on-going production in their factory. That's a great example of something that is obviously possible, that such things aren't utopian. That's why their story is
important to me, because I want it to be remembered and their
example to be talked about as much as possible. That's why I
really hope that it becomes a museum piece, because along with
that painting goes the story of their struggle, which should be
preserved for future generations.

Ivan: I have one more question. In the context of what you just
described, a new generation who will read the words next to the
painting and take in that message, we've discussed how these
are people from a generation who do not remember earlier eras.
But I wonder if it is realistic that this new generation will accept capitalists as businessmen or if a new type of hatred will
develop because no one likes to be degraded, even if that is how
they are taught. Or maybe a third possibility, and this is what
would be most dangerous, in which that exploited young worker moves to redress his grievances by competing to become his
boss; that this is his only goal, one completely devoid of historical experience.

Milica: I would say that it's not either-or. I'm imagining the future now, but it's not that hard to predict; it's enough to go to the US and to see how it has really functioned for years, a well-developed economic system. There are those who accept this as a given, who don't think about different starting positions; they simply think that that's how it is, like a birth right. Certainly there will be those who rebel. Some will undoubtedly direct their rebellion to becoming one of those who do the crushing, not one who is crushed. The US will sell the American Dream of potential success, which is of course an efficient means of pacifying people, through just that promise. Actual analysis and critique of the system is left to a very few people, who may uncover other alternatives through their investigation, but their level of influence is questionable.

Ivan: Is solidarity subversive these days?

Milica: Solidarity is, I think, always subversive, but it must be widespread to be subversive enough, but if it's there then it has immense strength.

Saša: In the composition of this painting, the colors and the overall artistic expression, did you try and depict your vision of the future, of society, some optimism or pessimism?

Milica: Well not consciously, but it was very interesting to me when during one of the tours through the exhibition, a man I didn't know but who turned out to be an art theorist began to read symbols and allegories in the painting of which I was completely unaware, and had not consciously brought to the painting. It turned out that those were things I added on to the original video still which served as the basis for the painting. He analyzed, for example, this knot/arrangement of hands and their inter-relation, and most interesting was that this woman in the first panel, he saw as freedom on the barricades, a woman as a symbol of the revolution, in a red shirt – workers' struggle, with hands arrayed like this, which he said represented victory or the like. So of course, there are certainly different readings of which I'm not aware, which should be inherent to any artistic work.

Saša: I wonder why this small section of the painting with many heads jammed together seems so dynamic and strong, as though from that corner comes something that will swallow everything else...

Ivan: They're coming....
Saša: ....very strong.
Ivan: ...unstoppable.
Milica: Well it may wind up like that, not just in your interpretation of this painting, but in the near future.

Serbia, *Zrenjanin, Jugoremedija* 2004.
Technique: acrylic on canvas (made by inmates in prison @ Sombor), framed with baroque frame. | Dimensions 287x213cm | 2010.

Zrenjanin, Jugoremedija, 2004
(2010 Notes about the cover painting)

ARTIST: MILICA RUŽIČIĆ
BACKGROUND TEXT WRITTEN BY IVAN ZLATIĆ

Pharmaceutical Factory Jugoremedija from Zrenjanin in Serbia was privatized in 2001 in such a way that the workers and retired workers got 58% and the state 42% of the shares. In 2002 the state sold its portion of shares to Jovica Stefanović – Nini, a businessman from Niš, who was still on the interpol's wanted list at that time as Smiljko Kostić's close associate in cigarette smuggling. In 2003 at the Jugoremedija Assembly, the small shareholders refused Nini's proposal to become the majority owner through recapitalization so he forged the decision on recapitalization, registered in court as the owner of 62% of the shares and started persecuting the workers that were active in the Trade Union and Small Shareholders' Association.

Notices given to two workers' leaders were the motive for the first strike in Jugoremedija in December 2003. At the beginning of January the strike was ended successfully and alongside their activities in the factory, the Association submitted the request for annulling the recapitalization. Stefanović disbanded the factory security, formed his private army in Jugoremedija and increased the pressure upon the workers, which provoked another strike in March. The workers threw the private security out of the factory, and Stefanović's management left Jugoremedija. During the following summer they tried to get in by force several times, but with no success. However, on August 19th Nini's private army provoked the fight with workers-shareholders again, which the police used as the reason to enter the factory area. Although the Zrenjanin police established order, the Government sent a paramilitary police unit from Belgrade, under the command of general-major Milivoje Mirkov, to Jugoremedija the same afternoon. In the evening Mirkov summoned four workers' leaders to the Zrenjanin police for negotiations. There he informed them they were arrested. They spent the following 10 days in isolation cells. Workers-shareholders, the majority owners of Jugoremedija, were thrown from the factory area on the 20th August. In spite of the public scandal caused by the brutality of paramilitary police forces, in spite of the Government Anti-Corruption Council's findings that the police should have maintained order in Jugoremedija, and not intervened in the property dispute that was being conducted in court, Stefanović continued with violence—he fired the workers that had been on strike. In the following year he bought Belgrade Serbolek, Menta from Padej… Wherever he came, he started plundering, selling goods to his companies at the reductions of over 30%. At the same time, 150 fired workers-shareholders of Jugoremedija were fighting persistently in public and in court for their right to live and work. In December 2006, the Supreme Court passed a judgment in their favor. Stefanović stayed in Jugoremedija for a whole three more months, trying to take raw materials and products from the warehouse in order to prevent small shareholders from restarting production after the takeover. The workers blocked the entrances and guarded the factory day and night until the 1ˢᵗ of March 2007, when at Jugoremedija Assembly more than 4000 small shareholders presented majority ownership and elected new management.

In the following three years, Jugoremedija workers-shareholders themselves, relying exclusively on their work and their own resources, invested over ten million Euros in bringing the production process into line with European standards. At the same time they supported the struggle of workers and small shareholders in several Zrenjanin companies that had similar problems in privatization, as well as numerous groups throughout Serbia, such as the workers in Zastava elektro, Trudbenik, Srbolek…

Stefanović continued with plundering and violence against workers and shareholders of the companies he was buying in privatisation processes. He was arrested on the 9ᵗʰ of November

2010 on charges of damaging the workers and shareholders of Srbolek of over five million Euros.

Milivoje Mirkov is retired now, and is a security commissioner of the Football Association of Serbia.

Created under the aegis of Servo Mihalj industrial complex in 1961, defended by workers' and share-holders' solidarity struggle, Jugoremedija has become the only company in Serbia where, through joint-stock company bodies, the spirit of genuine self-management has been created. Such probably did not exist at the time of official "self-management".

Paintings, on police brutality

The following pages offer black-and-white reproductions of Milica Ružičić' series of paintings on police brutality. This format does not do them "justice"—please visit our website at http://journal.radicalcriminology.org/ to see them in full (bloody, intense, living, breathing) color. In her introduction to a 2010 gallery exhibit, she says of this series:

> Following the news all over the world about the different protests and demonstrations that were suffocated by the police, I realized that the violence of the state is pretty much the same, although the states themselves look differently organized. What I would like to suggest by choosing these scenes is the question: By whose interests are the police guided in these cases?

> These news are visible but they are consumed fast and also forgotten quickly. That's why I wanted to put these pictures in media of painting on canvas. Painting is a medium that lasts much longer than photos in the newspapers or internet, especially if they are sold and then hung on a wall by the owner. Using them as evidence I didn't want to change anything but the background of each scene, which I left blank, symbolically unifying them. Titles of the paintings are the excerpts from the original news scenes are taken from.

▲ Greece, Athens 2008.

An officer was convicted of murder after the Athens death of
Alexandros Grigoropoulos sparked nationwide riots.

Technique: acrylic on canvas | Dimensions: 32x42cm | 2009.

▲ Bangladesh 2007.

Security agencies often intimidate, harass, detain
and torture journalists with impunity
despite continuous international protests.

Technique: acrylic on canvas | Dimension: 32x42cm | 2009.

▲ India, Bangladesh 2010.
Police using batons, tear gas and water cannons
fought street battles with 15,000 textile workers
demanding back pay and an immediate rise in monthly wages.
The workers currently earn a minimum monthly salary
of £15 and have demanded a 300 per cent raise.

Technique: acrylic on canvas | Dimension: 32x42cm | 2010.

▲ Germany, Heiligendamm 2007.

Demonstrations against G8 summit in Heiligendamm.
Member of special unit against riots in Germany,
unknown police officer has shown his cold-blooded
brutality on a young girl during arrest.

Technique: acrylic on canvas | Dimension: 32x42cm | 2009.

▲ Israel, Tel Aviv 2008.

Protest in Tel Aviv – of both Jews and Arabs –
against a reunion of Etzel, one of the terrorist Zionist groups used
against the Arab population in the process of the formation of the
state of Israel. In the "only democracy in the Middle East" these
peaceful demonstrators were brutally manhandled by the police.

Technique: acrylic on canvas | Dimension: 32x42cm | 2009.

▲ **Paraguay, Asuncion 2008.**
The police in front of the building of the State General Attorney brutally repressed protesters by beating them, spreading tear gas and shooting rubber bullets from very short distances, resulting in sixty people injured, including women and children.

Technique: acrylic on canvas | Dimension: 32x42cm | 2010.

▲ **Iran, Tehran 2007.**
Police brutality against low-level criminals accused of
alcohol-related charges as well as selling satellite dishes.

Technique: acrylic on canvas | Dimension: 32x42cm | 2009.

▲ Nepal, Kathmandu 2006.

Police in Kathmandu opened fire on tens of thousands of
pro-democracy protesters who defied a curfew to stage
a rally against the rule of King Gyanendra.

Technique: acrylic on canvas | Dimension: 32x42cm | 2010.

▲ **Kenya, Nairobi 2007.**
Anti-riot police during protests in the Nairobi's Kiera slum.

Technique: acrylic on canvas | Dimension: 32x42cm | 2010.

▲ Denmark, Copenhagen 2009.

Protests as a reaction to the Climate talks summit of UN. 986 were arrested without committing any offense and had been left to sit for hours in a freezing cold street.

Technique: acrylic on canvas | Dimension: 32x42cm | 2010.

▼ **Great Britain, London 2009.**
Protests against the G20 summit of the wealthiest states,
which generate global policy.

Technique: acrylic on canvas | Dimension: 32x42cm | 2010.

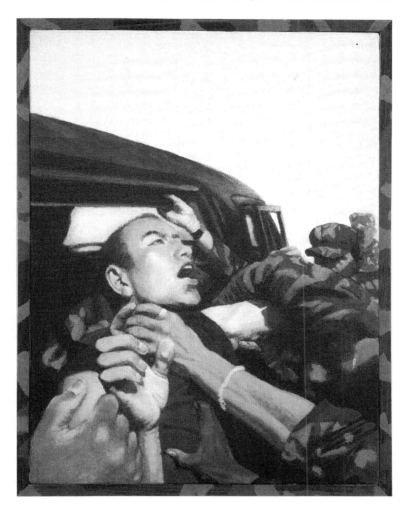

▲ Tibet, Lhasa 2008.

Chinese police arrest Tibetan monk. Around 130 people have been confirmed killed in a Chinese crackdown on protests and unrest in Tibet. (2010) The demand is urgent because China not only oppresses the Tibetan people, it is also destroying Tibetan culture.

Technique: acrylic on canvas | Dimension: 32x42cm | 2010.

▲ South Korea, Seoul 2003

South Korean workers and students clash with riot police after an anti government rally. Demonstrators from the Korean Confederation of Trade Unions and students took to the streets in Seoul to demand better working conditions and to protest the government's decision to send more troops to Iraq.

Technique: acrylic on canvas | Dimension: 32x42cm | 2010.

▲ Zimbabwe, Harare 2009.

Zimbabwean police officer about to forcefully use a
truncheon on a fleeing demonstrator at the anti-poverty
protests, organized by opposition to Mugabe regime.

Technique: acrylic on canvas | Dimension: 32x42cm | 2010

▲ Germany, Rostock 2007.

German police clashed with hundreds of protesters
in the port of Rostock, following a much larger peaceful
demonstration against Group of Eight summit
in a nearby Baltic resort.

Technique: acrylic on canvas | Dimension: 32x42cm | 2009.

▲ Australia, Sydney 2002.

Protests against the meeting of the World Trade Organization. Australian police went in hard against around 500 protesters, arresting 35. The police even used force to bust up the orderly departure of the demonstrators.

Technique: acrylic on canvas | Dimensions: 32x42cm | 2009.

□ ◇ □□ ◇ □□ ◇ □

Mandy Hiscocks was sentenced to spend most of 2012 in prison because of her participation in organizing against the G20 leaders summit in Toronto in the summer of 2010.

Her raw & gripping jail blog has touched thousands of readers, offering a powerful condemnation of the rotten Canadian criminal "justice" system, along with sharp insights to surviving the inside. With fierce unbroken defiance, she reminds us of the importance of maintaining our own dignity and integrity through whatever isolation and trials may come, and she underlines the significance & urgency of prisoner solidarity work.

Here's an excerpt of her reflection on "seasons and oak trees" ...

i want to tell you about a tree i've befriended. [...] there's a window in the hallway there that [...] looks out onto a huge, beautiful oak tree. i've been reading about oak trees recently, and why they have never been domesticated despite their tasty and nutritious acorns that have been both a staple and a fallback food for humans for thousands of years.[...] three reasons are given for humans' failure to accomplish this:

1) slow growth. it takes ten years or more for an acorn to grow into a productive tree;

2) by burying acorns squirrels disperse them far and wide, and when they forget to dig them up some will grow. because of all that wild, unmanaged planting going on humans would have an incredibly difficult time selecting only for the trees we want;

3) acorn bitterness is controlled by many different genes as opposed to a single dominant one. getting rid of a trait with diverse genetic causes is very difficult, so most acorns on any given tree would be bitter despite humans' best efforts to manipulate them.

i see an analogy to effective resistance here. slow and steady growth, wide and unmanaged spread of ideas ensuring that some take root, decentralized movements and diversity of tactics. . .i think the mighty oak might have a lesson for us! i like to think about this kind of thing as i admire the tall, ever wild tree outside the window. at the moment it's surrounded by concrete and fencing but it has never succumbed to human domination. i hope it lives to see this jail crumble to dust.

boredbutnotbroken.tao.ca

'Oak Tree' by Gedimin A Bulat

[insurgencies]

Repression, Resistance, and the Neocolonial Prison Nation

K.Kersplebedeb

In California, the past several months have witnessed one of the most impressive prison struggles in recent memory. For 21 days in July and 17 in September/October of 2011, thousands of prisoners participated in a hungerstrike against torture. Despite not winning all of their demands, the prisoners won politically, transforming the terrain on which they, and we, must organize our next move.

Prisoners in isolation at Pelican Bay State Prison's Security Housing Unit (SHU) had put out the word that they would be going on hungerstrike on July 1, news that traveled the length of the California system in the months beforehand. While their demands were specific to their own situation, they remained broad enough to reflect the reality of other prisoners held in isolation throughout California, and so individuals and then groups in other prisons began expressing that they too would be joining the hungerstrike. Men and women with different national and organizational affiliations promised to come together in unity behind these demands (listed in the sidebar).

STRIKES, RETALIATION, RESOLUTION

During the first week of the strike in July, over six thousand prisoners refused state meals. Some did eat food they had bought beforehand, some took only the liquid portion of their meal (i.e. juice or milk), while others refused any sustenance whatsoever. Regardless of the degree of participation, all were acting as part of a collective rising up, signaling their solidarity with those being held in long-term isolation.

It was the greatest challenge to the California prison system in recent memory.

The first strike lasted three weeks before a deal of sorts was struck. According to the prisoner representatives from Pelican Bay, the California Department of Corrections and Rehabilitation (CDCR) agreed to address all of the strikers' demands, and as a token of good faith agreed to immediately allow prisoners to buy warmer clothes, wall calendars, and to take classes with proctored exams. But as soon as the prisoners resumed eating, CDCR officials began to publicly distance themselves from this deal, stating instead that the agreement had only been for these "tokens of good faith," denying any commitment beyond that.

As a result, the Pelican Bay prisoners put out the call to resume their hungerstrike on September 26. Many observers expected this second strike to be more difficult, and smaller, than the first. It was feared that because the July strike had been called off with some confusion over what had or had not been won, that it would be more difficult to move people to put their lives on the line for a second time. What these fears did not take into account was the psychological terrain that had been liberated by the first strike, the sense of collective empowerment that resulted from the fact that thousands had together succeeded in drawing attention to the realities of life in California's isolation chambers.

When the second strike started in the last week of September, 12000 prisoners refused food, almost twice as many as during the summer.

Once again, after weeks of playing hardball, CDCR returned to the negotiating table, promising this time that within the next year they would review the cases of all prisoners held in the SHU. As a result, the second hungerstrike was called off on October 13.

During the course of these two strikes there were support demonstrations throughout California, and across the United States. This was centered around San Francisco, where the left has a considerable infrastructure built up, and spearheaded by an ad hoc Prisoner Hunger Strike Solidarity Coalition.[1] Over time, though, more and more support actions were taking place in Los Angeles, where the communities and families of many of the prisoners are to be found. Support activities also took place on the international stage, with vigils and demonstrations taking place from Montreal, Canada, to London, England. By the time of the second hungerstrike, Amnesty International was taking a public position calling "for urgent implementation by the California prison authorities of policies to improve conditions in, and assignment to, the state's Security Housing Units," and calling "on the Department of Corrections and Rehabilitation to ensure that prisoners seeking an end to inhumane conditions are not subjected to punitive measures."[2]

Despite this call, and unusually sympathetic coverage in the national media, hungerstrikers faced a variety of forms of repression, both during and after each strike.

Prisoners are one of the least healthy sections of the U.S. population, with many having chronic medical problems and special needs. One of the first things prison officials did was to state that those who were not eating would be denied their medication, on the grounds that medicine must to be taken with food. As Chad Landrum, who suffers from end-stage liver disease, recounted in a letter:

> In an effort to break my strike they began withholding my pain medication as leverage. At first cold turkey until I reminded them of the *Plata* and the federal judge's ruling that it is criminal to cold turkey a long-time recipient of medications for chronic pain. So they issued just enough to clear them, but so minute and ineffective to cause extraordinary pain, from both disease and withdrawal symptoms. When that failed they came to my cell and said I need to go to the CTC [infirmary] because I'm so sick and totally disabled [...] Well, in an effort to "help me" and ensure my dire health needs are met, when I refused to go they extracted me. A very brutal act. They did not enter as I prepared for, but instead, with three types of "toys", an overwhelmingly suffocating gas, or like an impenetrable cloud or fog, filled my cell. Then they tossed in a type of gas bomb. Then hit me with a direct spray of another gas. On the verge of passing out I left the cell. Interestingly, all the taunting and provok-

[1] See: http://prisonerhungerstrikesolidarity.wordpress.com/
[2] "USA: Amnesty International calls for urgent reforms to California security housing units as prison hunger strike resumes" accessed at http://www.amnesty.org/en/library/asset/AMR51/085/2011/en/fb49a11e-6b06-47c5-8379-97051bab6247/amr510852011en.html

ing challenges [by guards] abruptly ended when the video camera arrived.

"What happened to me," Landrum observes, "was wrong on so many levels."

In some prisons, hungerstrikers were also denied liquids. For instance, at Calipatria, during the second strike prisoners had been clear in all of their declarations that they were on a "solid food only strike", by which they meant that they were only refusing solid foods. Located at the southern end of California, Calipatria houses many prisoners awaiting transfer to Pelican Bay. Facing desert temperatures on the Mexican border, prisoners intended to continue accepting the liquid portion of their meals. Nevertheless, they were not only denied such liquids but the water in their cells was also turned off for hours at a time. Despite this, it looked like the Calipatria prisoners would continue the second strike even after the Pelican Bay representatives had struck a deal; at that point the warden announced that if they did so not only would they be refused their medications as well as liquids, but so would all other prisoners, including those who were not on hungerstrike. Faced with this threat, the Calipatria prisoners called off their strike.

This was not the only escalation during the second strike. Lawyers from California Prison Focus and Legal Services for Prisoners with Children, who had actively visited with hungerstrikers during the first strike, were now barred from entering prisons and threatened with investigation for "jeopardized the safety and security of CDCR" institutions.[3] In prisons across California, hungerstrikers were denied their right to visits or yard time. In an attempt to foster tensions in the general prison population, it was threatened that non-striking prisoners would also be locked down. In many prisons those suspected of being hungerstrike leaders were thrown into solitary. At Pelican Bay's SHU, where prisoners are already in solitary, hungerstrikers were removed to the Administrative Housing Unit where their isolation continued, only now with air conditioning

---

[3] Prisoner Hunger Strike Solidarity, "CDCR Threatens Crackdown of Prisoner Hunger Strike, Bans Lawyers: Mediation Team Appeals to Governor for Action," Press Release, September 30, 2011. Accessed at http://prisonerhungerstrikesolidarity.wordpress.com/cdcr-threatens-crackdown-of-prisoner-hunger-strike-bans-lawyers-mediation-team-appeals-to-governor-for-action-2/

left on at maximum 24-hours a day. As Chad Landrum, one of those moved to the ASU, explained: "It freezes 24 hours a day and you are entitled only to the linen on your bed, what's on your back, and a towel." The *New York Times* quoted one striker, Ronald Yandell: "It's like arctic air coming through, blowing at top speed. It's torture. They're trying to break us."

Such retaliation, along with the actual health effects of not eating, did take a toll, and in both the summer and the fall, the numbers on strike began to decline sharply after the first week. Nevertheless, in each case, hundreds of prisoners continued to refuse food for the full course of the action, and had no agreement been reached, several indicated that they were willing to die.

PELICAN BAY: THE EYE OF THE STORM

It surprised no one that the epicenter of this struggle was to be found at the extreme northern tip of California, at Pelican Bay prison's notorious Security Housing Unit. There should be no mistake: this is a torture unit, the site of an unabashed behavior modification program, all conducted under cover of containing "gangs".

Prisoners at the SHU live alone in 8'x10' cells. The lights are kept on 24 hours a day, and there is no natural sunlight. Unlike most prisons, no phone calls are allowed nor can prisoners have photos taken to send to their loved ones. Any visits that are approved must take place through a glass partition, and are restricted to 90 minutes and only on weekends. Allowed out of their cells for less than two hours a day, prisoners spend this time – alone – in what the prison refers to as the "exercise yard"; in reality simply a larger cell with grating on the ceiling. Needless to say, there is no exercise equipment provided. The only time SHU prisoners might see one another is at the law library, other than that life is spent in total isolation. Even shouting out to one another through the slot that is used to deliver food can be considered engaging in "gang communication", and may be used as a pretext to add years onto one's time in the SHU.

According to Craig Haney of the University of California Santa Cruz:

there is not a single published study of solitary or supermax-like confinement in which nonvoluntary confinement lasting for longer than 10 days, where participants were unable to terminate their isolation at will, that failed to result in negative psychological effects. The damaging effects ranged in severity and included such clinically significant symptoms as hypertension, uncontrollable anger, hallucinations, emotional breakdowns, chronic depression, and suicidal thoughts and behavior.[4]

Haney's own research at Pelican Bay, published in 2003, found that

virtually all of the isolated prisoners were plagued by nervousness and anxiety, by chronic lethargy, and a very high percentage (70%) felt themselves on the verge of an emotional breakdown. In addition, a very high number suffered from headaches and troubled sleep, and more than half were bothered by nightmares. Well over half of the supermax prisoners reported a constellation of symptoms - headaches, trembling, sweaty palms, and heart palpitations - that is commonly associated with hypertension.[5]

What's more

Almost all of the supermax prisoners reported suffering from ruminations or intrusive thoughts, an oversensitivity to external stimuli, irrational anger and irritability, confused thought processes, difficulties with attention and often with memory, and a tendency to withdraw socially to become introspective and avoid social contact. An only slightly lower percentage of prisoners reported a constellation of symptoms that appeared to be related to developing mood or emotional disorders - concerns over emotional flatness or losing the ability to feel, swings in emotional responding, and feelings of depression or sadness that did not go away. Finally, sizable minorities of supermax prisoners reported symptoms that are typically only associated with more extreme forms of psychopathology - hallucinations, perceptual distortions, and thoughts of suicide.[6]

It is important to appreciate the fact that these torturous conditions are not the result of some accident, oversight, budgetary constraints or simple ignorance on the part of prison administrators. The conditions at Pelican Bay's SHU, and other isolation units across the United States, were carefully crafted with the goal of breaking prisoners' minds while withstanding any legal challenges. Isolation torture was scientifically developed in the postwar era, generally targeting small numbers, often po-

---

[4] Haney, Craig "Mental Health Issues in Long-Term Solitary and 'Supermax' Confinement," *Crime & Delinquency* 2003 49, p. 132.
[5] Haney, p. 133.
[6] Haney, p. 134.

litical prisoners. In Europe, the most (in)famous experiments in this vein occurred in Northern Ireland and West Germany. In the United States, scientific interest in using prisons to conduct such programmes was evident in the early sixties,[7] though the most obvious forerunners of today's SHUs were Marion prison and the Lexington High Security Unit in the 1980s. These conditions were then refined and replicated in a wave of control unit construction in the late 80s and early 90s. In the words of political prisoner Bill Dunne, this "inaugurated an age of escalating ruling class resort to this qualitatively higher level of repression aimed at more class-interest effective use of the prison system, the leading edge of the apparatus of social control."[8] (Dunne, serving an over-100-year long sentence for attempting to break a comrade out of prison, can attest to this personally: he was at Marion in the 80s, and is presently buried in a Communications Management Unit in Pollock, Louisiana.[9])

Today, control units like the SHU are an integral aspect of America's system of mass incarceration.

According to CDCR, the SHU holds "the worst of the worst", hardened gang leaders who would otherwise engage in violence against other prisoners. In fact, though, most prisoners in the SHU are there for administrative, not disciplinary reasons. Their "gang" label is not based on any behaviour, but on profiling and association. A typical example: in the 2009 court ruling *Lira vs. Cate*, it was found that former prisoner Ernesto Lira had spent years in the SHU because of a sketch he had allegedly drawn, an anonymous tip, and a report from a prison guard that was mis-transcribed. The court found that as a result of his time in the SHU, Lira now suffers from post-traumatic stress disorder and clinical depression, and that throughout his incarceration, despite his objections that he was not a gang-

---

[7] Dr. Mutulu Shakur, Anthony X. Bradshaw, Malik Dinguswa, Terry D. Long, Mark Cook, Adolfo Matos, James Haskins, "A Scientific Form of Genocide," in *Let Freedom Ring*, pp. 73-5.
[8] Dunne, Bill "Strings Attached in the Age of Authority," in *Let Freedom Ring*, p. 110.
[9] As of Sept. 2010, according to Denver ABC, his address is: Bill Dunne, #10916-086 USP POLLOCK U.S. PENITENTIARY P.O. BOX 2099 // POLLOCK, LA 71467

member, he was never provided with any meaningful review of his "validation".[10]

Other prisoners end up at the SHU as retaliation for lawsuits against CDCR, or for organizing with other prisoners, or for their political beliefs. As Sanyika Shakur, a New Afrikan Communist, and author of the bestselling book *Monster: The Autobiography of an L.A. Gang Member*, explained in a letter shortly before the first hungerstrike:

> The CDC cited writings i had from Comrade-Brotha George, exercising in military fashion with known revolutionaries & conducting joint military manoeuvres with other formations in the New Afrikan Independence Movement. i came up for an "inactive" review in 2008, but the political police said my name was found on a roster of known & active members of various formations in the cell of a New Afrikan on San Quentin's death row. For this & writing "Black August" in a letter, i was given an additional six years in the SHU, on an indeterminate status.[11]

The NCTT-COR-SHU prisoners' collective at Corcoran recently provided another example of such political profiling:

> a debriefer who was briefly in this individual's cell told I.G.I. [the Institutional Gang Investigator] the individual spoke of the merits of socialism, the history of political resistance to racism in America, and the validity of the socio-economic and political views of Frantz Fanon, Ho Chi Minh, and George Lester Jackson. The I.G.I. told the debriefer this was "B.G.F. [Black Guerilla Family] education", to which the debriefer quickly agreed, framed it in those terms, and parroted what his I.G.I. handler told him to. Now this same guy the debriefer was lying on wrote an article in *California Prison Focus* in 2003 critical of CDC, its use of validation on political + politicized prisoners and some leftist political ideas. They considered <u>this</u> "more than one source independently provid[ing] the same information" and part of the information provided by the source has already proven to be true. They of course gave him a "1030" for the article itself, 5 years old, at that same time for "providing BGF education" in a *California Prison Focus*. This expression of his political views and social criticism of CDCR's practice of arbitrarily targeting and punishing left wing political ideologues in prison, in violation of the 1st Amendment and California Code of

---

[10] *Lira v. Cate*, 2009 U.S. Dist. LEXIS 91292 (N.D. Cal. Sep. 30, 2009). See also Carbone, Charles "The Jailer Has No Clothes" *California Prison Focus* #34 pp 13-4 accessed at http://prisons.org/documents/CPF-34.pdf

[11] "Sanyika Shakur, August Third Collective, On July 1 Hunger Strike", see http://www.kersplebedeb.com/mystuff/july1/june_sanyikashakur.php

Regulations Title 15 §3004, was sufficient to earn him an indefinite continuation in SHU.[12]

Many people end up in the SHU because of what an informant says about them. There is no trial, or chance to appeal. As prisoner representative George Franco has explained

> I been in on an indeterminate SHU since beginning of 1992. For conspiracy to commit harm to others safety. This info was given by informant(s). Every six yrs I could appear before a committee to see if I'm eligible for the six yrs. non-active so that I can be sent to a mainline but before this six yr. period an institutional gang investigator (IGI) with search property in cell and for some reason will al-ways use something a picture, drawing, pattern, address plus some so called valid info to use to extend the six yr non-active period all over again. It's a cycle we all go through. If I choose to debrief: snitch-rat I would be let out to a mainline but that is not my belief. I would never have a person put in SHU. So like I said only option to get out of SHU is either snitch, die or parole.

Indeed, turning people into informants is the stated goal of confinement in the SHU. Snitching on other prisoners or associates on the outside is referred to as "debriefing", and for administrative SHU prisoners it is the only way back to general population.

These are the conditions against which the prisoners went on hungerstrike. While CDCR's agreements do not entail dismantling the SHU or an end to abusive use of anti-gang measures, these must be seen as the only longterm goals worth pursuing. By coming together in collective action as they did this year, the California prisoners have taken an important step in that direction.

While Pelican Bay's SHU is one of the most infamous control units, such facilities exist across the United States. Most state prison systems have one or more control units, referred to as "segregation units", "high security units", "special handling units" and a variety of other names. On the federal level, there are several Communications Management Units, housing mainly Muslim prisoners incarcerated during the so-called "War on Terror". Add to this the isolation wings and "holes" within prisons throughout the country, and it has been estimated that at

---

[12] NCTT-COR-SHU, "A Brief Discussion on the Reality and Impact of SHU Torture Units in the Wake of the August 23rd Legislative Hearings" accessed at http://www.kersplebedeb.com/mystuff/july1/sept_nctt.php

any one time over 100,000 prisoners are being held in some form of solitary confinement.

Not only are the numbers of people in isolation unprecedented, but so is the amount of time spent in such conditions. At Pelican Bay, where 1,111 people are in held in the SHU, less than 100 have been there for less than five years; 513 have spent more than a decade in isolation, 78 have spent twenty years or more. Long-term isolation is in fact a reality across the United States, one often directed specifically at political prisoners. Some examples: Herman Wallace and Albert Woodfox, along with Robert King, had organized the first prison chapter of the Black Panther Party, in 1971. They were subsequently framed for the murder of another prisoner, and have been held in solitary confinement ever since. Hugo Pinell was one of the San Quentin Six, charged with murder and conspiracy following the assassination of George Jackson by guards in 1971. Pinell was found guilty of assault, and has been held in solitary for the past forty years—since 1989 at Pelican Bay. Russell Maroon Shoatz was a soldier with the Black Liberation Army, and managed to escape from prison twice in the 1970s—he has been held in solitary confinement for over 21 years now, despite recommendations from the Pennsylvania Department of Corrections that he be released into general population.

These are just a few of the many political prisoners who are subjected to these conditions in the hopes of either coercing them to renounce their beliefs, or destroying them psychologically. Ralph Arons, the former warden at Marion in the 1980s, was blunt about this goal, testifying in court that, "The purpose of the Marion Control Unit is to control revolutionary attitudes in the prison and in society at large." At Lexington's High Security Unit at the same time, political prisoner Susan Rosenberg and POW Alejandrina Torres were each told by unit director Ogden that they would be released into general population only if they renounced their views.

Indeed, as the Committee to End to Marion Lockdown wrote in 1987:

> Although the government denies the existence of political prisoners in this country, it often reserves the harshest treatment for these very people. Control Units are designed to break every prisoner's spirit. In the case of political prisoners and prisoners of war, the

Control Units are part of a calculated strategy to weaken these movements and to intimidate others from taking a stand.[13]

Bringing such pressure to bear on political prisoners is one part of the state's counterinsurgency strategy against the liberation movements. A corollary to this targeting of revolutionaries is the identification and targeting of those segments of the population that revolutionary movements have emerged from historically. In the United States, this means the internal colonies: Indigenous nations, Puerto Rico, Aztlan, New Afrika. If the first aspect counterinsurgency warfare took the form of COIN-TELPRO and political imprisonment, the second took the form of mass incarceration, as colonized communities found themselves newly criminalized, with millions of their members now slated to spend decades of their lives behind bars.

As Michelle Alexander concludes in her 2010 book *The New Jim Crow:*

> Saying mass incarceration is an abysmal failure makes sense, though, only if one assumes that the criminal justice system is designed to prevent and control crime. But if mass incarceration is understood as a system of social control— specifically, racial control —then the system is a fantastic success.[14]

Control units such as the Pelican Bay SHU are emblematic of both aspects of the state's relationship to oppressed communities and the liberation movements that have emerged from them. As such, in their struggle against isolation, the California hungerstrikers have underscored a connection between prisoners who may have different pasts, but whose futures promise to share much in common. They have struck a blow on behalf of all prisoners' rights, and indeed, on behalf of the rights of all of us who may some day end up in prison – and as Chad Landrum wrote shortly before the second hungerstrike

> Rights are relative, they are in a constant state of transformation and change, of perpetual transition. There are no such thing as rights, there are only power-struggles. The moment we cease to struggle, we cease our claim to rights. All who can be mobilized, stand up! Unite![15]

---

[13] Committee to End the Marion Lockdown, "The People's Tribunal to Expose Control Units" Let Freedom Ring p. 95.

[14] The New Jim Crow, p. 225.

[15] Landrum, Chad "A Statement and Call for Mutual Support in Unity" September 23, 2011 accessed at

THE 5 CORE DEMANDS OF THE PELICAN BAY SHU HUNGER STRIKERS**

1. **End Group Punishment & Administrative Abuse**—
This is in response to PBSP's application of "group punishment" as a means to address individual inmates rule violations. This includes the administration's abusive, pretextual use of "safety and concern" to justify what are unnecessary punitive acts. This policy has been applied in the context of justifying indefinite SHU status, and progressively restricting our programming and privileges.

2. **Abolish the Debriefing Policy, and Modify Active/ Inactive Gang Status Criteria**—
   - Perceived gang membership is one of the leading reasons for placement in solitary confinement.
   - The practice of "debriefing," or offering up information about fellow prisoners particularly regarding gang status, is often demanded in return for better food or release from the SHU. Debriefing puts the safety of prisoners and their families at risk, because they are then viewed as "snitches."
   - The validation procedure used by the California Department of Corrections and Rehabilitation (CDCR) employs such criteria as tattoos, readings materials, and associations with other prisoners (which can amount to as little as greeting) to identify gang members.
   - Many prisoners report that they are validated as gang members with evidence that is clearly false or using procedures that do not follow the Castillo v. Alameida settlement which restricted the use of photographs to prove association.

3. **Comply with the US Commission on Safety and Abuse in America's Prisons 2006 Recommendations Regarding an End to Long-Term Solitary Confinement**—

---

http://www.kersplebedeb.com/mystuff/july1/sept_landrum.php

CDCR shall implement the findings and recommendations of the US commission on safety and abuse in America's prisons final 2006 report regarding CDCR SHU facilities as follows:

• End Conditions of Isolation (p. 14) Ensure that prisoners in SHU and Ad-Seg (Administrative Segregation) have regular meaningful contact and freedom from extreme physical deprivations that are known to cause lasting harm. (pp. 52-57)

• Make Segregation a Last Resort (p. 14). Create a more productive form of confinement in the areas of allowing inmates in SHU and Ad-Seg [Administrative Segregation] the opportunity to engage in meaningful self-help treatment, work, education, religious, and other productive activities relating to having a sense of being a part of the community.

• End Long-Term Solitary Confinement. Release inmates to general prison population who have been warehoused indefinitely in SHU for the last 10 to 40 years (and counting).

• Provide SHU Inmates Immediate Meaningful Access to: i) adequate natural sunlight ii) quality health care and treatment, including the mandate of transferring all PBSP- SHU inmates with chronic health care problems to the New Folsom Medical SHU facility.

4. Provide Adequate and Nutritious Food—
cease the practice of denying adequate food, and provide a wholesome nutritional meals including special diet meals, and allow inmates to purchase additional vitamin supplements.

• PBSP staff must cease their use of food as a tool to punish SHU inmates.

• Provide a sergeant/lieutenant to independently observe the serving of each meal, and ensure each tray has the complete issue of food on it.

• Feed the inmates whose job it is to serve SHU meals with meals that are separate from the pans of food sent from kitchen for SHU meals.

5. Expand and Provide Constructive Programming and Privileges for Indefinite SHU Status Inmates—

Examples include:

• Expand visiting regarding amount of time and adding one day per week.

• Allow one photo per year.

• Allow a weekly phone call.

• Allow Two (2) annual packages per year. A 30 lb. package based on "item" weight and not packaging and box weight.

• Expand canteen and package items allowed. Allow us to have the items in their original packaging [the cost for cosmetics, stationary, envelopes, should not count towards the max draw limit]

• More TV channels.

• Allow TV/Radio combinations, or TV and small battery operated radio

• Allow Hobby Craft Items – art paper, colored pens, small pieces of colored pencils, watercolors, chalk, etc.

• Allow sweat suits and watch caps.

• Allow wall calendars.

• Install pull-up/dip bars on SHU yards.

• Allow correspondence courses that require proctored exams.

**as signed by

Todd Ashker	Arturo Castellanos
Sitawa N. Jamaa (s/n R.N. Dewberry)	George Franco
Antonio Guillen	Lewis Powell
Paul Redd	Alfred Sandoval
Danny Troxell	James Williamson
Ronnie Yandell	*...and all other similarly situated prisoners*

Date: April 3, 2011

◻ ◊ ◻◻ ◊ ◻◻ ◊ ◻

Prison Expansionism, Media, and "Offender Pools": An Abolitionist Perspective on the Criminalization of Minorities in the Canadian Criminal Justice System

STEVEN NGUYEN

Increases in prison construction under Stephen Harper's Conservative government pave the way for an ever-expanding prison population followed by a persistently growing pool of offenders to ensure prison beds will be filled. This phenomenon of prison expansionism is outlined in Thomas Mathiesen's (1986) classical text on abolitionism. Informed by Mathiesen's argument of prison expansionism this paper will explore the role of mass media in conjunction with the criminalization of minorities which ensures a constant pool of offenders to supply the much-needed bodies for prison consumption.

Mathiesen points out the expansionist characteristic of prison construction, referring to two types: prison substitutes and prison additions (Mathiesen, 1986). Although, as Mathiesen (1986) points out, there is a greater tendency for prison additions because prisons constructed as substitutes rarely result in the replacement or closing of older, outdated prisons: they continue to stand and function (1986, 91). As Justin Piche shows, provincial governments have constructed twenty-two new prisons accompanied by seventeen prison additions from 2007 to the present; during this same period there have been thirty-four additions to federal prisons (Piche, 2011). The construction of prisons will naturally increase the capabilities of government to house more offenders. This increase in prison beds begets a subsequent increase in potential "offenders" to

131

draw from within the general population to meet this increasing need. The role of the mass media to propagate messages of criminality to the general public is vital in this process.

Mathiesen illustrates the dangerousness of the "new media" and points out how we have become dependent on media institutions for "definitions, significance, and response" (1986, 85). The operation of the media to "prime audiences" serves to reinforce specific messages about race and criminality to the general population (Jiwani 2011, 45). Working alongside priming is the use of "media templates" to simplify analysis of news stories to ameliorate misunderstandings the general population possess regarding news events (Jiwani 2011, 45). Stereotypes and racial profiling are the trademarks of the mass media, aiding to criminalize those outside of the mythical norm.

The social construction of criminal populations stands in juxtaposition to the mythical norm, defined on the basis of race, sex, age, sexual orientation, religion, and economic position (Perry 2011a; 2011b). This construction is further refined by Lorde:

> Somewhere, on the edge of consciousness, there is what I call a *mythical norm*, which each of us within our hearts knows "that is not me". In America, this norm is usually defined as white, thin, male, young, heterosexual, Christian and financially secure. It is with this mythical norm that the trappings of power reside within this society. (quoted in Perry 2011a, 19)

Those blessed by fate to possess characteristics of the mythical norm become the standard to which all are judged. Fiske (1996) suggests that "whiteness is exnominated," whereby the characteristic of whiteness is the "normative background against which others are defined and their differences rendered salient" (quoted in Jiwani 2011, 41–42). It becomes clear that those who deviate from said norms become easy targets of criminalization and incarceration. There is no greater example than black Canadians and their treatment by criminal justice agencies because of the mass media.

The media play an influential role in defining the criminality of black Canadians. Wortley (quoted in Wortley and Owusu-Bempah 2011) suggests that black Canadians are vulnerable to media depictions as criminal offenders rather than victims of crime. These depictions of black criminality primes the populace, reinforcing stereotypical notions of black behaviour and

criminal tendencies. These sterotypes often manifest in "popular culture [films, music, etc]" (Wortley and Owusu-Bempah
2011, 130). The role mass media play in disseminating information will strongly influence public opinion.

The stereotypes propagated by the mass media depicts and
demonizes entire black communities based on the actions of a
few Wortley and Owusu-Bempah 2011). Entire communities
are seen as "foreign" or "alien" (Wortley and Owusu-Bempah
2011, 130). This process of demonization has serious negative
consequences, as Wortley and Owusu-Bempah observe: "the
negative impact that racialized images of crime can have on the
black community is evident in the results of public opinion
polls" (2011, 130). These polls found that half of Ontario residents believe in a strong relationship between race and crime
(Wortley and Owusu-Bempah 2011, 130). Police officers are
as much affected by media stereotypes as any other member of
the population. These processes result in differential treatment
of black Canadians by the gatekeepers of the criminal justice
system.

Racial profiling has been defined by Wortley & Tanner
(2003; 2004; 2005), and Harris (2002) as "(1) significant racial
differences in police stop and search practices; (2) significant
racial differences in Customs search and interrogation practices; and (3) particular undercover or sting operations that target specific racial/ethnic communities" (quoted in Wortley &
Owusu-Bempah 2011, 135). These differential treatments of
black Canadians based on media-driven stereotypes create an
"offender" population to fill the expansion and construction of
prisons. Not all black members of a community will commit
crimes. Indeed, as Wortley and Owusu-Bempah (2011) suggest, the practice of racial profiling "may help explain why
black people comprise the majority of people charged with drug
crimes in North America, even though criminological evidence
suggests that the majority of drug users and sellers are white"
(2011, 137). These practices of increased surveillance increase
the odds that a black person will come into contact with the
gatekeepers of the justice system to ensure a consistent flow of
"offenders" headed towards incarceration. Once entered into
the system black Canadians also experience differential treatment by the judiciary.

Although there is a lack of comprehensive research in Canada regarding sentencing for minorities who victimize white people, American research strongly suggests that "regardless of their own race, individuals who victimize white people are sentenced more harshly by the courts than those who victimize blacks and other racial minorities" (Cole 1999, quoted in Wortley and Owusu-Bempah 2011, 141; Spohn 2000; Johnson 2003; Urbina 2003). Differential sentencing against a multicultural backdrop, such as Canadian society, ensures prison beds remain occupied by racial and ethnic minorities. So long as racial and ethnic minorities continue to receive differential treatment by the criminal justice system, the prisons will continue to have a pool of socially constructed offenders to draw upon. Black Canadians have served this role for the state well but the scope of surveillance and security has expanded its focus towards other immigrant populations as well.

Mass media communication technologies serve a vital role in (mis)characterizing immigrants. Media typographies arranging and ordering information in a specific way reinforce notions of criminality among these newly arriving populations. Jiwani's analysis of Toronto *Globe and Mail* newspaper headlines illustrates this point: the majority of headlines pertaining to Middle Eastern countries relate to terrorism and Al-Qaeda, while other immigrant nations are highlighted with violence, corruption, and gangs (2011, 47). The connection between immigrants and crime is due to "media-driven moral panic" (Costelloe 2009, quoted in Ismaili 2011, 94). Moral panics aim to hide underlying societal issues by scapegoating marginalized members of a population as a threat to the social order. Moral panics effectively utilize populace support for government-based programs which seek to deny accused individuals by restricting their rights and placing them under surveillance and control.

Immigrants have historically been the targets of moral panics, even though the expansionist culture of prisons that Mathiesen (1986) spoke of had not yet been established. The Opium Act of 1908 criminalized otherwise law-abiding Chinese Canadian workers under the guise of morality (Zong and Perry 2011). Chinese Canadians, hardworking and underpaid, became the focus of security and became criminalized under the moral panics of that era. The new, present-day moral panic has expanded its focus from Chinese workers and fixated upon religious minorities.

Islamophobia, defined by the British Runnymede Trust, is "the dread or hatred of Islam and therefore the fear and dislike of all Muslims" (quoted in Helly 2011, 164). These attitudes are based on:

> four main negative stereotypes...[manipulated] by politicians, intellectuals, journalists, and pressure groups: (1) Islam is an intolerant and even dangerous religion; (2) democracy and modernity are impossible in Islamic societies; (3) women's oppression is inevitable in Islam; and (4) immigrant Muslims are archaically religious and beset by the conflicts of their societies of origin. (Helly 2010b, quoted in Helly 2011, 170)

These attitudes towards Muslim immigrants stem from media coverage's "mediocre analysis of socio-political contexts in foreign countries and... ignorance of the cultures and opinions of immigrants from those countries" (Helly 2011, 171). The effects of biased media coverage have impacted Canadian attitudes spanning from the West to the East; many Canadians "wanted to see a reduction in immigration from Islamic countries" (Helly 2011, 170). These attitudes would have drastic effects when coalesced with government policies, and administered to place immigrants from Islamic countries under surveillance, control, and incarceration.

The events of 9/11 changed the world, egregiously impacting Muslim immigrants. As Helly reminds us, Muslims were quickly criminalized with the passing of the Anti-Terrorism Act, among other similar legislations (2011, 178). In Canada, the Anti-Terrorism Act expanded police powers, allowing them to perform secret searches, listen in during conversations between individuals, and perform secret investigations under the guise of fighting terrorism (Helly 2011). As absurd as these practices appear, the use of security certificates has amounted to atrocious violations of human rights against suspected individuals.

Security certificates allow for the prolonged detention of Muslim immigrants with no obligation on the state to convict (Helly 2011). Muslims detained under these certificates lacked the "procedural safeguards respected in a democratic state" such as the disclosure of evidence, public trial, appeal, etc.

(Helly 2011, 178). The issuance of security certificate feeds the prison expansionist paradigm by detaining individuals for long periods of time, often without the consultation of legal aid, and offers very little chance for victims to defend themselves. Lacking protective measures against state control targeted people of Muslim background and future immigrants deemed a threat to the social order, real or perceived, will continually provide physical bodies to meet the needs of the prison expansionist beast. Alongside this continuum of racial and immigrant "offender" populations, the scope of authoritarian powers to surveil and incarcerate continues to expand, seeking to place more members of the population under its criminalization paradigm.

There must be alternatives to the the expansion of incarceratory practices and validating prison constructions. Huslman's (1986) analysis of crime and our conception of responses provides an appropriate base to begin our discussions on alternatives to penality. Drawing on the work of Black (1976) and Meclintock (1980) Huslman applies person oriented and structure oriented responses to social conflict (quoted in Hulsman 1986, 73). These responses of social control include: "penal, compensatory, therapeutic, conciliatory, and educational" (Hulsman 1986, 73). Hulsman (1986) provides a deeper analysis to these styles of resolving conflict in his work, but it suffices to say there are many alternatives to our formal mode of punitive punishment: the criminal justice system. Though such informal modes may appear unapplicable in our highly securitized society, such reforms are the basis of negative reforms advocated by Mathiesen (1986) and other abolitionists.

Meaningful change will depend on how we choose to respond to social conflicts between racial and ethnic communities, and also how we deal with the dissipation of community and family relations. These changes must occur within the panopticon of a mass media institutions which promote stereotypes and biases; the emergence of a new, independent media must be pursued. The dissemination of evidence-based perspectives underscoring compassion and understanding towards criminalized members of the population must be consciously addressed. Finally, we must cease the propagation of fear, instead choosing to foster empathy and knowledge, and in doing so undermine prison expansionism to return "offender" populations back into the community of human beings.

REFERENCES

Harbison, J. 2011. "Older People, Crime, and State Intervention." In *Diversity, Crime, and Justice in Canada*, ed. B. Perry. Don Mills: Oxford University Press, 253–277.

Helly, D. 2011. "Justice and Islam in Canada." In *Diversity, Crime, and Justice in Canada*, ed. B. Perry. Don Mills: Oxford University Press, 164–186.

Hulsman, L. H. 1986. "Critical Criminology and the Concept of Crime. *Contemporary Crises* 63–80.

Ismaili, K. 2011. "Immigration, Immigrants, and the Shifting Dynamics of Social Exclusion in Canada." In *Diversity, Crime, and Justice in Canada*, ed. B. Perry. Don Mills: Oxford University Press, 89–105.

Jiwani, Y. 2011. "Mediations of Race and Crime: Racializing Crime, Criminalizing Race." In *Diversity, Crime, and Justice in Canada*, ed. B. Perry. Don Mills: Oxford University Press, 39–56.

Mathiesen, T. 1986. "The Politics of Abolition." *Contemporary Crises*, 81–94.

Perry, B. 2011a. "Framing Difference." In *Diversity, Crime, and Justice in Canada*, ed. B. Perry. Don Mills: Oxford University Press, 16–38.

Perry, B. 2011b. "The Mythical Norm." In *Diversity, Crime, and Justice in Canada*, ed. B. Perry. Don Mills, Ont: Oxford University Press, 57–70.

Piche, J. 2011. "Tracking the Politics of 'Crime' and Punishment in Canada." *TCPC-Canada Blogspot*. Retrieved December 4, 2011. http://tpcp-canada.blogspot.com/2011/04/considering-abolition-notes-for.html

Wortley, S. and A. Owusu-Bempah. 2011. "Crime and Justice: The Experiences of Black Canadians." In *Diversity, Crime, and Justice in Canada*, ed. B. Perry. Don Mills: Oxford University Press, 125–148.

Zong, L. and B. Perry. 2011. "Chinese Immigrants in Canada and Social Justice: From Overt to Covert Racial Discrimination." In *Diversity, Crime, and Justice in Canada*, ed. B. Perry. Don Mills: Oxford University Press, 106–124.

SUPPORT POLITICAL PRISONERS

**Check the web for local groups
doing prisoner support in your area...**

prisonjustice.ca
abcf.net &
  BristolABC.wordpress.com
  DenverABC.wordpress.com
  GuelphABC.noblogs.org
  TorontoABC.wordpress.com
4strugglemag.org
supportmariemason.org
supporteric.org

FELLOW WORKERS:

Remember!

WE ARE IN HERE FOR YOU; YOU ARE OUT THERE FOR US

GDC

Books 2 PRISONERS

PRISONJUSTICE.CA

[book reviews]

The Red Army Faction—A Documentary History. Vol. I: Projectiles for the People
Smith and André Moncourt (Eds),
(Montreal: PM Press, 2009).

Reviewed by—Guido G. Preparata,
Kwantlen Polytechnic University, March 2012

This first installment of the documentary history of the Red Army Faction by J. Smith and A. Moncourt is a hefty tome of nearly 700 pages, which covers the vicissitudes of Germany's most famous terrorist outfit. The historical segment under review is the "classic" septennium: 1970-1977. This, indeed, was a time when the world at large seemed to have been invested by a wave of metropolitan counterinsurgency movements— from Latin America to Turkey and Japan by way of Europe, with Germany and Italy as its two most salient manifestations. The simultaneousness and similitude of such socio-political phenomena across geographical and cultural divides was, to put it mildly, uncanny. In this regard, the seventies were a unique period, and the detailed chronicles variously compiled of the strife that shook the constituted order in several nations at the time make up dazzling and forbiddingly complex material—material whose interpretative key social scientists and historians alike have been striving to discover ever since.

Complex material in that, much like the now-faded (and far from fully understood) tales of late-XIXth century "anarchism," the rebellious actions of these masked sappers of the urban un-derbrush —pre-modern or post-modern— could never be quite construed as simple, obvious strikes at the most conspicuous

(physical and/or institutional) symbols of the "system."
Through their deeds, these guerrillas might have thought they
were propitiating full-scale revolution, but seen from a distance,
their agitation seemed rather to have weighed as yet another
variable in a larger equation. Not only were the vast majority of
terrorist cells subject to standard life-cycles and reorganization
processes—e.g., an old guard superseded by a more militant
and violent "second wave" (and sometimes, a third and fourth
wave)—, but their offensive patterns were also too heteroge-
neous, their strategies too mutable over time, and their targets
too specific to have made terrorism's enterprise, in the final
analysis, a simple expression of (class) warfare seeking to reform "the capitalist system." In other words, terrorism is not
merely the extreme embodiment of economic grieving —and of
its concomitant political disaffection—but is rather a matter of
politics, of power. At the grassroots levels, most of these movements of urban warfare had emerged during the turbulent paren-
thesis of the Counterculture era (late sixties), yet they eventually survived, evolved and morphed into ever more elusive apparatuses—not few of them with unfathomable international rami-
fications— at a time when the popular ferment that birthed
them had virtually disappeared (mid-seventies).

Originally tuned in the key of social justice, subsequently
bolstered by choreographed violence, and finally deployed on
the chessboard as a full-fledged political player, (Left-wing)
terrorism confronts us defiantly with its mysteries. So we wonder, what is/was terrorism? And, to retrace the notable an-
tecedents, what was the RAF, in essence?

Smith and Moncourt's volume is a very valuable resource in
this regard: it is compilation of the most significant tracts of the
paper trail left behind by the organization during its first and
defining seven years: manifestos, interviews, communiqués,
letters and all manners of invectives penned by the RAF's
members, friends and foes. To have all such "originals" in one
book, complemented by a meticulous chronology is special indeed: one may excavate, re-appraise the old revolutionary lin-
go, and even attempt to guess the sentimental contours of that
distant, strange world by nosing into the (often inflamed) letters
the guerrillas would write to one another in and from jail. The
book is organized chronologically in fifteen chapters, from the

immediate postwar era to 1977—that is to the conclusive year of the RAF's "historical" phase, which itself comprised two sub-periods: that of the so-called original nucleus of Baader-Meinhof (1970-1972), and the second wave of 1975-1977. Each chapter is prefaced by a deeply researched study of the editors, who frame the chronicle of the armed struggle in its socio-cultural context: cumulatively, such introductory labor takes approximately a third of the book—it is thus substantial and particularly informative.

As said, and as is the case for most flamboyant terrorist cells, the mere storyline of the RAF—its characters, the military "spectacles," the incarcerations and mysterious deaths—is in itself particularly gripping: cinema-worthy indeed, as shown by the recent release of *The Baader-Meinhof Complex* (2008). In synthesis, this is the story of an original core of rebellious types who had risen to front the violent, illegal vanguard of the most recalcitrant wing of the students' anti-imperialist movement. These types were animated by palingenetic *furore* and driven by a *keen death-wish*—for such seems to have always been the psycho-sociological template of the "average" urban guerrilla; Baader had sentenced: "We are a projectile." The highlights of this "baptismal" phase (consummated between 1970 and 1972) were feats of arson; bombing attacks (the 1972 "May Offensive") against two NATO bases in West Germany, which altogether claimed the lives of 4 US soldiers, and other domestic targets, including the emblematically conservative Springer press; and the armed rescue of the charismatic leader Andreas Baader (May 1970) by his confederates, a mere month after his forcible detention (on charges of arson). These beginnings drew to a close as all the historical figures of the RAF were, by July 1972, apprehended one by one, amidst a frazzling whirl of incidents. Chief among these incidents were putative State-provocations—i.e. "false-flag" operations, hoaxes, and the like, all of them designed to foment a state of collective dementia praecox and reinforce the Establishment thereby—as well as the hunting down and eventual killing by police forces of RAF fighters in broad daylight. And to crown it all, it so seemed that throughout this interlude that RAF had moreover availed itself of an intriguing connection to the Stasi, the odious secret police of the GDR—connection which seemed to account for the organization's fluid use of the international *réseau* that would put it in operational contact with other European and Palestinian terrorist squads.

With the definitive demise of the "old guard" began the second and far more puzzling, as well as disquieting, act of the narrative. To begin, these founders of the RAF, under what appeared to be a studiously torturous and dehumanizing regime of imprisonment, were on the other hand *publicly* recast as waxen icons of the militant Left—icons which the authorities, with a developed sense of museological theatrics, proceeded to encase into the ultra-modern carcerary shrine of Stammheim. From there, in semi-effigy, they were to "radiate" their iconic strength to the outer rims of West Germany's Marxist-Leninist subversion and inspire its militants with renewed revolutionary ardor. While this set-up was being completed, the recruits of the "new" RAF, including the auxiliary phalanx of another terrorist clan—the Movement of the 2nd June (2JM)—were preparing the second grand offensive of 1975-1977. This sensational offensive would feature the abduction of Christian-Democrat politico and mayoral candidate for W. Berlin, Peter Lorentz (February 1975), and his subsequent release in exchange for a group of political detainees flown on the occasion from West Germany to Yemen; the takeover of the West German embassy in Stockholm (April 1975); the assassination of Attorney General Siegfried Buback (April 1977) and of banker Jürgen Ponto (July 1977); and, the high climax of this progression: the kidnap and ensuing assassination of the industrialist Hans-Martin Schleyer, in concomitance with the hijacking of a Lufthansa aircraft by a Palestinian commando—a spectacular move improvised to ante-up the RAF's request to swap Schleyer with the inmates of Stammheim (September-October 1977). Refusing to negotiate on behalf of Schleyer, the executive of Helmut Schmidt eventually managed to retrieve the hostages by dispatching a Special Force commando to storm the plane, which, in the course of a veritable and tragic odyssey, had been ultimately diverted to Mogadishu. The morning following the day of the rescue operation (October 17), the authorities announced that the bodies of Baader & co. had been found (gruesomely) "suicided" in their cells at Stammheim, and on October 19 the RAF led the police to a car in the city Mulhouse, near the German border, in whose trunk lay the bullet-ridden corpse of Schleyer.

All of which is here recited to emphasize, by way of summary, that the RAF's is indeed an extraordinary, and extraordinarily mysterious, story. And all of it is recounted with captivating rhythm in this book. Clearly, in no fashion does this summary exhaust the many themes of the narration; one can dig in the book so much more: viz., the socio-economic portrayal of Germany during reconstruction; the very interesting description of West Germany's anti-parliamentarian, *spontaneous* scene; the retelling of the late post-modern drift of the West-German Left into feminism and environmentalism; the genealogy of notorious political figures of our time from the turbulent seeds of the seventies (e.g., Gerhard Schröder and Joschka Fischer); the *fundamental* role of "the lawyer" in these games of terror/power, and the enigmatic trajectories that some of these lawyers did take (the fascinating case of Horst Mahler, from RAF counsel to Holocaust Negationist); and finally, not to be missed, that surreal anecdote of the terrorists' brains removed before burial and handed over to the clinicians of Tübingen with a view to discover, in the worst Lombrosian manner, a lesion that could "scientifically" account for the revolutionists' moral insanity (a vignette, by the way, that elicits a twisted reminiscence of Kaspar Hauser's autopsy...).

To return to the point previously made about terrorism being a game of power, what seems to be somewhat lacking from this otherwise notable collection is precisely the *political* commentary, i.e. the sub-text of "deep politics." In this respect, Smith and Moncourt confine themselves to the traditional explanations of radical economistic theory, according to which modern society is divided into a capitalist elite and a majority of (subdued) subjects. The subjects, de facto, are depicted as (indentured) servants of this elite that coerces them daily via a strict diet of hard power (physical intimidation, if need be) and a multi-layered fare of soft-power stimulants, of which the circus and the bread-line remain the foundational archetypes. It follows that if such is the realm we are given to live into, social justice can only be achieved by means of resistance, or defiance, which, ultimately, signifies struggle. Violent struggle, that is. Adopting the leftist historiographical stance, Smith and

Moncourt maintain that the FRG was in actuality nothing but a repressive technocracy erected, under the American aegis, upon the foundations of the former Nazi Behemoth. In light of this, any kind of resistance—even, if not especially, armed resistance—was entirely justified in their view. Clearly, the authors feel admiration and—as they retell their gestes—root for the fighters of the RAF, making no mystery of their sympathies, which go out not just to the idealist *guerrilleros* of the Marxist left, but to all armed rebels of the "undogmatic Left." In this sense, this book is also very much a paean sung for all those insubordinate types that have categorically refused, often paying with their life, to adapt to a mode of life that so completely antagonized their moral sense and deepest psychic and sentimental affects.

Needless to say, the issue of justice in this world and the challenge of coping with the strictures of collective life, especially for those who happen to have been born on the wrong side of the fence (the vast majority of the world population), is not just the crux of political philosophy broadly defined, but is one of the questions that impinge on the very meaning of life itself. Vast problem. I do not wish to dispute the validity of radicalism's basic premises—namely, that the world is for the most part organized upon the exploitation of the peaceable by the barbarous, and that the peaceable must "resist" somehow. It may very well be so. But the vexed question is what forms this resistance should take, and in the name of which principles. As said, Smith and Moncourt have no doubt. The impassioned, if not exceedingly "youthful," tone of their narrative conveys the message without ambiguity: the struggle should be fierce for it is clear that right always lies on the side of the Left's "steadfast combatants"—heroic guerrillas who, in the editors' words, will always be countered by the "vulgar" and underhanded brutality of the "cops" and the "dirty play" of their capitalist paymasters in the government.

Now, I find this sort of approach problematic for two orders of reasons. First, advocacy of violence is always dangerous: one, simply because it is immoral, and, two, because many of those who care about the fate of social justice no less strongly than the authors, are instinctively repulsed by the language and praxis of violence, which, as we all know, are the defining expressions of the exploitative mindset we all wish to resist in the first place. It's an old story, of course: that of the young, tormented idealist that wants to change the world, finds out he cannot, and so reverts to conservatism; an old story that has covered vast expanses of discursive production, some of which keeps returning to various modules of Machiavellian resignation (think of Julien Freund and others). Leaving for the moment this daunting preoccupation aside, and without further digressing, it should nonetheless be stated that the primary objective of a movement for civil dissent is to keep its feet on the ground, not to hearken impulsively to the (now totally vanished and positively perplexing) heyday of Baader & Co, and never stop thinking of peaceable ways in which to implement social reforms.

Secondly, and more to the point, to treat the historiography of the RAF according to this "us vs. them" format does not add much, if anything, to the mainstream (i.e. conservative) version of these events—i.e. to the very mainstream version that Smith and Moncourt's have designed to challenge with their prefatory scholarship. It is as if we are re-viewing the same reel but with a different soundtrack, punctuated this time around by cheers rather than boos: yet the plotline remains as impenetrable as ever. Because Smith and Moncourt should know, in fact, that it is *unthinkable* that a fistful of death-prone, yes, but not particularly intelligent, resourceful or talented twenty-somethings (and the "first" RAF even had a sixteen-year-old recruit!) could, by the skin of their teeth, hold in check or merely defy, for almost a decade, something as formidable as the apparatus of a modern bureaucratized State such as the FRG. Obviously, they were (sacrificial) pawns in a bigger game. Everything indeed, points in this direction: their remarkable connection to the Stasi and Palestinian terrorism; the particular timing of the bombing campaigns and of the arrests; the whole circus macabre of Stammheim; the essential spin of the media, the function of the latter as sounding board of the terrorist antics, and the central role played in this regard by *Der Spiegel*; the surgical targeting of Buback, Ponto and Schleyer; and, last but certainly not least, that sensational coda of the Schleyer/Mogadishu *affaire*. How can all this boil down to a simple tale of urban revolt for fairer economics?

Holding on to their economistic mold, the authors do not provide a theory that explains consistently, and in keeping with the political evolution of the West German scene in the context of the Cold War, the true strategic motivations behind this sequence of terrorist maneuvers. This brings them, for instance, to dismiss the Stasi-connection and the financial/logistical support that came with it, as something utterly marginal and almost mischievously intended "to get at the Americans." But, evidently, it was neither. Likewise, in their view, Ponto was obviously assassinated because he had financial ties to Third World tyrants (and the Apartheid); and Schleyer was obviously kidnapped (and then killed) because, having once fought in the SS, he was "the most powerful businessman in West Germany at the time," and like, Ponto, "a frequent figure on television representing the ruling class point of view" (p. 477). But was Schleyer really West Germany's most powerful businessman? How "powerful," and in what sense, exactly? And, is it not rule n. 1 for *truly* powerful people never to appear, least of all on television?

And, in truth, what was there to gain, *for the revolution, concretely*, by bombing a supermarket or NATO headquarters, or by singling out and liquidating, say, a high-level businessman or banker, even assuming (erroneously) that he was so "powerful" as to be irreplaceable? Nothing —and there is the rub of the entire matter: that the illusion entertained by all guerrillas (at least officially) to fire up the masses with such inciting murders was just that. It was *never* a possibility in the early days when the fires of protest were still smoldering, and, as mentioned above, it had become a total delusion by the mid-seventies: from the outset, the "angry ones," the potential rioters without any stake in conformity, had always been far too few to spark anything even remotely resembling the mass uprising they were all dreaming of.

In sum, the analysis suffers somewhat not only from a disregard of the wider political landscape of that era, but also from the candor of taking events at *face value*: politics is also theatrics, and terrorism/urban guerrilla warfare, by definition, is certainly not the weapon the weak wield against the powerful, but, rather, an instrument of (civil) conflict which the powerful, when sundered in factions, employ to fight one another by using (a particular typology of) the weak. Even after all the painstaking and precious work of historical reconstruction of the RAF's experience, such as has been carried out also in this volume, there still remains, in the end, to solve the whole mystery. The questions to be asked are thus: who/what was maneuvering these expendables in this complex game of murder and provocation, and to what end?

Freedom Not Yet: Liberation and the Next World Order.
Surin, Kenneth.
(Durham: Duke University Press, 2009, 415 pp.).

Reviewed by—Jeff Shantz,
Kwantlen Polytechnic University, March 2012

Despite spectacular failures (most recently the financial crisis of 2008 to present) neoliberalism continues to dominate the policy visions and commitments of global decision-making elites. Opposition to neoliberal politics and the possibilities of social transformation and the development of real alternative social relations are at the heart of heterodox Marxist Kenneth Surin's concerns in *Freedom Not Yet*. Surin (who has previously made some useful contributions to autonomist Marxist theory) suggests that within projects of Western neoliberalism most people are in need of liberation from their socioeconomic circumstances. Neoliberalism creates an increasingly polarized and impoverished society. Surin is particularly interested in the oppression of poorer countries and the poor globally. He asks:

"Who are the political subjects capable of building and maintaining a liberated world? What are the possibilities of their development as forces for social change?"

Surin notes that political innovation, and the alteration of politics, is required to achieve social liberation from neoliberal capitalism. In his view, part of this innovation includes drawing upon the insights of contemporary (post-modern) philosophy. In this regard he draws upon the works of Badiou, Žižek, Deleuze, and Negri among others.

Freedom Not Yet is divided into three primary sections. The first examines the current regime of accumulation, particularly the financialization of capital. The second section looks at the constructions of subjectivity and identity and the reproduction of people as social beings within specific contexts. The third section addresses liberation and the prospects for alternative notions of subjectivity that might move beyond the limited (and cynically deployed) notions of humanism as motivated within liberal democracies (14).

At the same time, Surin argues for the continued importance of Marxist theory which remains, in his view, indispensable. Surin seeks the philosophical possibilities of a Marxist or neo-Marxist perspective on liberation from capitalist regimes of economic exploitation and political domination. As a Marxist, Surin is concerned first with understanding the economic relations that structure the present period. He starts his work with an analysis of the current regime of accumulation.

Neoliberalism includes the domination globally of financial markets, investment, and speculation over traditional production economies (as under industrialism or secondary sector dominance). The domination of financial markets is enacted partly through neoliberal social policies that subordinate poor people and poorer economies to the priorities of capitalist markets and trade. Surin is also concerned with the neoliberal constitution of subjectivity—the creation of neoliberal subjects for whom neoliberalism is regarded simply as a "way of life," the only possible world. The production of neoliberal subjects is a key aspect of contemporary struggles over dispossession and exploitation, for Surin.

Unlike many post-Marxist theorists who, over the last few decades of "end of history" defeatism in Marxist circles, have given up hopes for revolutionary transformation and turned instead to social democracy (so-called "radical democracy"), Surin seeks the conditions and prospects for revolution in the twenty-first century. From a Marxist perspective, Surin argues that economic crises, such as the current financial crisis of 2008 to the present, are results of the structures of capitalist development, of regimes of production and accumulation. For Surin, the financial crisis is the product of deep tensions within the capitalist system of accumulation which can only be removed through removal of the system that produced, and continues to produce, them in the first place (1). This distinguishes him from other critics—liberal, conservative, postmodern and post-Marxist alike—for whom the question of capitalism as a system of accumulation to be superceded is largely avoided or discounted.

For Surin, 1989 and 2001 provide key dates in the periodization of the symbolic history of neoliberalism. 1989 signaled, of course, the collapse of the Soviet regimes as well as the final years in office of Reagan and Thatcher, whose mythologies of the renaissance of the US and Britain as the "rightful" world powers provided impetus for the rule of "free market values" and the demise of social welfare (and social movements). Notably, the collapse of distinctions between left and right, and the loss of belief in possibilities of revolutionary transformation, became widely entrenched after the collapse of the Soviet forms of "communism" after 1989. The other symbolic date is 9-11, 2001. This moment has served as the mobilizing myth behind the recent nationalist and expansionist drives to war and occupation and the US pursuit of global geopolitical domination.

The Reagan-Thatcher project was a response to the decline of the period of postwar economic growth (roughly 1945–1975). The neoliberal ideology, that was part of a broader structural adjustment project, offered several diagnoses for the collapse of the postwar boom—all of which were viewed as systemic. The pillars of neoliberal mythology involved attempts to overcome the supposed imposition of market rigidities, always attributed to the purported power or interference of labor unions, government regulation, "unfair" tax burdens on entrepreneurs who were presented as the real engines of the economy, and the excessive costs (in capital's view) of welfare systems that had among their imagined faults the creation of a "culture of poverty" which removed incentives for the working class to accept work in lower paying jobs, with little or no security. Indeed, these were the very work conditions sought by the budding entrepreneurs with their service sector economies (2). These pillars all remain as part of current political and economic discourses, even if some of the rough edges have been smoothed down (such as the most virulent attacks on single moms under popular Reagan and Bush discourses).

The task for neoliberal governments has been, and continues to be, the removal of the supposed market rigidities, government regulations and interventions in social welfare. Governments are said to exist to create or expand markets and protect property (militarily as well as judicially), especially from movements of the working classes and poor. Nothing more. The catchwords are deregulation and privatization. Notions of equality are reduced to an "equality of opportunity" that refuses even minimal efforts toward any actual redistribution of income (unless it goes from poor to wealthy).

In fact, despite the claims of neoliberal mythologizing, neoliberalism has actually been effected through what might be called more appropriately a "Military Keynesianism." While claiming to desire "less government" or "smaller government," ruling parties from Reagan through Obama and Thatcher through Cameron have massively grown the military and police functions of the state, at enormous cost, operating staggering deficits and running up record debts (as did the Reagan administrations, despite recent Republican revisionism). Neoliberal governments also, despite the mythology, have worked to centralize government, reaching the heights of executive exercise of authority as practiced under Bush the Younger. In addition, despite the anti-welfare bootstrapping rhetoric of successive administrations, neoliberal governments have also increased tax cuts, public grants, and interest free loans to corporations. What some term "corporate welfare," these polices have effected a massive transfer of wealth upward from poor to rich. Never mind the usual complaints about wealth redistribution offered by neoliberal parties.

The political outcome of neoliberalism has been the reduction of political action to the spectacle of mass media panics, poll chasing, and public relations focus group driven "issues management." A range of moral panics (typically centered around the poor and working classes) have been, and continue to be, regularly deployed to excite the electorate. So-called terrorists and "illegal" migrants have formed some of the most popular recent manifestations. Homeless people, "squeegee youth," and "riot grrls" posed some of the earlier examples. The hegemony of neoliberalism among parties of both left and right constructs politics as a matter of "positioning conformist citizens in front of the market" (9).

Under such conditions politics lost much meaning and distinctions between left and right, in mainstream party politics, dissolved in the electorally strategic, and highly profitable, pursuit of the marketable "centrist" position. Politics has been evacuated under economic managerialism and the forever deferred promise of trickle down economics that over time increases in wealth for the rich will filter down somehow to the poor. This approach, of course, has actually increased wealth even more for the already rich while devastating the poor and their communities.

Notably, the purportedly alternative politics of Clinton and Blair, supposed liberals, actually served to consolidate and extend the Reagan-Thatcher projects, making them more palatable (at least initially) to working class voters (4). Many disappointed liberals and social democrats are beginning to realize that Obama represents a similar "alternative" politics (or Trojan horse neo-liberal).

For Surin, the current period requires nothing less than a new democratic project. As he argues: "What is desperately needed today, therefore, is a new sociopolitical settlement, at once practical and theoretical, that will reclaim the political for the project of a democracy that will place the interests of the dispossessed at its heart" (11). To his credit, Surin sees this new democracy as being possible only as a project of liberation from the dispossession and exploitation that are at the center of capitalist structures of domination and power. It is his attempt to sketch the contours of liberation through postmodern Marxist theory that is less convincing and, finally, less promising than his approach first hinted at.

Surin notes that a key feature of the rise of neoliberalism has been the failure or problematization of categories of class struggle. Notions of social class and class struggle have clearly been marginalized throughout the last three decades. This marginalization has been deepened in media manipulated politics of the neoliberal period. The need for categorical innovation provides impetus for Surin's work. Marxism requires a renovation of its own categories and the current period of crises provides some encouragement for that effort within Marxism. Yet Surin, despite his recognition that the bureaucratic, centralized state (of Sovietism and corporatism) has had its day, maintains his Marxist belief in the need for a state apparatus to manage affairs, even in a liberated society. In the end he desires only a politics to the left of social democracy, but his vision is not clearly articulated. Disappointingly he calls for little more than a "vigorous democratization of our economic and political institutions" (15). This is extremely limited. The real issue is the existence of those institutions themselves, not their democratization.

Similarly disappointing is Surin's narrow appeal for "mechanisms of accountability" that cannot be bought off by the wealthy (15). The real questions are power, access, decision-making (and, indeed, property and wealth) rather than the return of regulatory bodies (that might again degenerate in the face of the above structures).

As well, Surin seeks a return of party politics not run by political "experts" and public relations managers. He seeks parties based on commitment "to substantive ideological positions" (15) and expressing differences between right and left that might better reflect the electorate's aims. This is once again the party politics of different parts that still make up the same whole (with loyal oppositions of left and right). Yet the real problem is party politics, representative democracy, and the domination of politics by professional organizations. The real problems might be understood as authoritarianism and statism, which create, maintain, and thrive on the dispossession that Surin is concerned with. Even when discussing the need for a strengthening of communal bonds in the US, Surin sees this as being beneficial largely in contributing to increased involvement in electoral politics.

The great need that Surin identifies, but does not satisfactorily explore, is the crucial need for the development and extension of bonds of community solidarity in the West, particularly the US and Canada. Yet this is not fully explored in his work. In my view, there is a real need for liberation movements in the West to build what I prefer to call infrastructures of resistance. These are the institutions and shared resources that might sustain communities and movements in struggles over time. There is little institutional analysis in Surin's work, either of the decline of previous infrastructures of resistance within the working classes (unions, mutual aid societies, flying squads, workers centers) or of emerging alternatives and their promise and prospects for continued development.

Given the stated goal of examining prospects and possibilities, as well as pathways, for liberation of the world's poor from conditions of poverty and dispossession, the philosophical examinations of Badiou, Derrida and others reads like a considerable detour. It is not that philosophy is unimportant or that the identified theorists do not offer some insights into the issues. It is more that the dense philosophical examinations in this volume do not seem to make much of a contribution to real world questions of liberation, dispossession, or resistance.

There is a disjuncture between the social scientific or political economic analysis in the first section—which is forcefully presented—and what seems to be a retreat into philosophical excursis. The chapters on philosophical writers read too much like overviews of each theorist's position. Noticeable is the nearly complete absence of any engagement with the political theorizing, strategies, or tactics produced and debated within contemporary movements and by activists and organizers. This is finally not even a book of the radical imagination, of the images, hopes, and desires that motivate or inspire political actors, movements or communities.

Radical Criminology, a new journal of theory and practice for struggle

Considering contributing to an upcoming issue?

Authors are encouraged to submit articles for publication, directly to our website:
http://journal.radicalcriminology.org

We are actively seeking marginalized voices, not only in the field of critical criminological scholarship, but also artists, activists, and reviewers.   Or, send us a letter!

All academic articles are subject to a blind peer review process. (This does not include "insurgencies," artwork, poetry and book reviews, which will be assessed by our editorial committee.)

Please visit our website for more detailed submission guidelines. (There are no submission nor publication fees.)

We use the Public Knowledge Project's 'open journal' online submission system (http://pkp.sfu.ca/ojs), which allows authors to submit papers via the Web. This system speeds up the submission and review process, and allows you to view the status of your paper online.

Artwork, poetic submissions, and notes on insurgencies can also be posted to our website, e-mailed to <editors@radicalcriminology.org> or send us mail at:
Radical Criminology,
ATTN: Jeff Shantz, Dept. of Criminology,
Kwantlen Polytechnic University
12666 72nd Ave,
Surrey, B.C. V3W 2M8